THE NATURAL HOUSE

FRANK LLOYD WRIGHT

THE NATURAL HOUSE

HORIZON PRESS   NEW YORK

CONTENTS

LIST OF ILLUSTRATIONS

FRONTISPIECE—FRANK LLOYD WRIGHT

BOOK ONE: 1936 – 1953

ORGANIC ARCHITECTURE

The typical American dwelling of 1893 was crowding in upon itself all over the Chicago prairies as I used to go home from my work with Adler and Sullivan in Chicago to Oak Park, a Chicago suburb. That dwelling had somehow become typical American architecture but by any faith in nature implicit or explicit it did not belong anywhere. I was in my sixth year with Adler and Sullivan then, and they had completed the Wainwright Building in St. Louis, the first expression of the skyscraper as a *tall* building. But after building the great Auditorium the firm did not build residences because they got in the way of larger, more important work. I had taken over dwellings, Mr. Sullivan's own house among them, whenever a client came to them for a house. The Charnley house was done in this way. I longed for a chance to build a sensible house and (1893) soon free to build one, I furnished an office in the Schiller Building and began my own practice of architecture. The first real chance came by way of Herman Winslow for client. I was not the only one then sick of hypocrisy and hungry for reality. Winslow was something of an artist himself, sick of it all.

What was the matter with the typical American house? Well, just for an honest beginning, it lied about everything. It had no sense of unity at all nor any such sense of space as should belong to a free people. It was stuck up in thoughtless fashion. It had no more sense of earth than a "modernistic" house. And it was stuck up on wherever it happened to be. To take any one of these so-called "homes" away would have improved the landscape and helped to clear the atmosphere. The thing was more a hive than a home just as "modernistic" houses are more boxes than houses. But these "homes" were very like the homes Americans were making for themselves elsewhere, all over their new country.

Nor, where the human being was concerned, had this *typical* dwelling any appropriate sense of proportion whatever. It began somewhere way down in the wet and ended as high up as it could get in the high and narrow. All materials looked alike to it or to anything or anybody in it. Essentially, whether of brick or wood or stone, this "house" was a bedeviled box with a fussy lid; a complex box that had to be cut up by all kinds of holes made in it to let in light and air, with an especially ugly hole to go in and come out of. The holes were all "trimmed"; the doors and windows themselves trimmed; the roofs trimmed; the walls trimmed. Architecture seemed to consist in what was done to these holes. "Joinery" everywhere reigned supreme in the pattern and as the soul of it all. Floors were the only part of the house left plain after "Queen Anne" had swept past. The "joiner" recommended "parquetry" but usually the housewife and the fashionable decorator covered these surfaces down underfoot with a tangled rug collection because otherwise the floors would be "bare." They were "bare" only because one could not very well walk on jig-sawing or turned spindles or plaster ornament. This last limitation must have seemed somehow unkind.

It is not too much to say that as a young architect, by inheritance and training a radical, my lot was cast with an inebriate lot of criminals called builders; sinners hardened by habit against every human significance except one, vulgarity. The one touch of nature that makes the whole world kin. And I will venture to say, too, that the aggregation was at the lowest aesthetic level in all history. Steam heat, plumbing, and electric light were the only redeeming features and these new features were hard put to it to function in the circumstances. Bowels, circulation, and nerves were new in buildings. But they had come to stay and a building could not longer remain a mere shell in which life was somehow to make shift as it might.

When I was 11 years old I was sent to a Wisconsin farm to learn how to really work. So all this I saw around me seemed affectation, nonsense, or profane. The first feeling was hunger for reality, for sincerity. A desire for simplicity that would yield a broader, deeper comfort was natural, too, to this first feeling. A growing idea of simplicity as organic, as I had been born into it and trained in it, was new as a quality of thought, able to strengthen and refresh the spirit in any circumstances. Organic simplicity might everywhere be seen producing significant character in the ruthless but harmonious order I was taught to call nature. I was more than familiar with it on the farm. All around me, I, or anyone for that matter, might see beauty in growing things and, by a little painstaking, learn how they grew to be "beautiful." None was ever insignificant. I loved the prairie by instinct as itself a great simplicity; the trees, flowers, and sky were thrilling by contrast. And I saw that a little of height on the prairie was enough to look like much more. Notice how every detail as to height becomes intensely significant and how breadths all fall short. Here was a tremendous spaciousness needlessly sacrificed, all cut up crosswise or lengthwise into 50-foot lots, or would you have 25 feet? Reduced to a money-matter, salesmanship kept on parceling out the ground, selling it with no restrictions. Everywhere, in a great new, free country, I could see only this mean tendency to tip everything in the way of human occupation or habitation up edgewise instead of letting it lie comfortably flatwise with the ground where spaciousness was a virtue. Nor has this changed much since automobilization has made it no genuine economic issue at all but has made it a social crime to crowd in upon one another.

By now I had committed the indiscretion that was eventually to leave me no peace and keep me from ever finding satisfaction in anything superficial. That indiscretion was a determination to search for the *qualities* in all things.

I had an idea (it still seems to be my own) that the planes parallel to the earth in buildings identify themselves with the ground, do most to make the buildings belong to the ground. (Unluckily they defy the photographer.) At any rate, independently I perceived this fact and put it to work. I had an idea that every house in that low region should begin *on* the ground, not *in* it as they then began, with damp cellars. This feeling became an idea also; eliminated the "basement." I devised one at ground level. And the feeling that the house should *look* as though it began there *at* the ground put a projecting base course as a visible edge to this foundation where, as a platform, it was evident preparation for the building itself and welded the structure to the ground.

An idea (probably rooted deep in racial instinct) that *shelter* should be the essential look of any dwelling, put the low spreading roof, flat or hipped or low gabled, with generously projecting eaves over the whole. I began to see a building primarily not as a cave but as broad shelter in the open, related to vista; vista without and vista within. You may see in these various feelings all taking the same direction that I was born an American child of the ground and of space, welcoming spaciousness as a modern human need as well as learning to see it as the natural human opportunity. The farm had no negligible share in developing this sense of things in me, I am sure.

Before this, by way of innate sense of comfort, had come the idea that the size of the human figure should fix every proportion of a dwelling or of anything in it. Human scale was true building scale. Why not, then, the scale fixing the proportions of all buildings whatsoever? What other scale could I use? This was not a canon taught me by anyone. So I accommodated heights in the ⇐ new buildings to no exaggerated established order nor to impress the beholder (I hated grandomania then as much as I hate it now) but only to comfort the human being. I knew the house dweller could seldom afford enough freedom to move about in built-in or built-over space, so, perceiving the horizontal line as the earth line of human life (the line of repose), this, as an individual sense of the thing, began to bear fruit. I first extended horizontal spacing without enlarging the building by cutting out all the room partitions that did not serve the kitchen or give needed privacy for sleeping apartments or (as in the day of the parlor) serve to prevent some formal intrusion into the intimacy of the family circle. The small social office I set aside as a necessary evil to receive "callers," for instance. Even this one concession soon disappeared as a relic of the barbarism called "fashion"; the "parlor."

To get the house down to the horizontal in appropriate proportion and into quiet relationship with the ground and as a more humane consideration anyway, the servants had to come down out of the complicated attic and go into a separate unit of their own attached to the kitchen on the ground floor. They liked this compulsion, though the housewife worried. Closets disappeared as unsanitary boxes wasteful of room and airy wardrobes in the rooms served instead.

Freedom of floor space and elimination of useless heights worked a miracle in the new dwelling place. A sense of appropriate freedom had changed its whole aspect. The dwelling became more fit for human habitation on modern terms and far more natural to its site. An entirely new sense of space values in architecture began to come home. It now appears that, self-conscious of architectural implications, they first came into the architecture of the modern world. This was about 1893. Certainly something of the kind was due.

A new sense of repose in flat planes and quiet "streamline" effects had thereby and then found its way into building, as we can now see it admirably in steamships, airplanes and motorcars. The age came into its own and the "age" did not know its own. There had been nothing at all from overseas to help in getting this new architecture planted on American soil. From 1893 to 1910 these prairie houses had planted it there. No, my dear "Mrs. Gablemore," "Mrs. Plasterbilt," and especially, no, "Miss Flattop," nothing from "Japan" had helped at all, except the marvel of Japanese color prints. They were a lesson in elimination of the insignificant and in the beauty of the natural use of materials.

But more important than all, rising to greater dignity as idea, the ideal of plasticity was now to be developed and emphasized in the treatment of the building as a whole. Plasticity was a familiar term but something I had seen in no buildings whatsoever. I had seen it in *Lieber Meister's ornament only. It had not found its way into his buildings otherwise. It might now be seen creeping into the expressive lines and surfaces of the *buildings* I was building. You may see the appearance of the thing in the surface of your

*Louis Sullivan

18

hand as contrasted with the articulation of the bony skeleton itself. This ideal, profound in its architectural implications, soon took another conscious stride forward in the form of a new aesthetic. I called it *continuity*. (It is easy to see it in the "folded plane.") Continuity in this aesthetic sense appeared to me as the natural means to achieve truly organic architecture by machine technique or by any other natural technique. Here was direct means, the only means I could then see or can now see to express, objectify and again bring natural form to architecture. Here by instinct at first (all ideas germinate) principle had entered into building as the new aesthetic, "continuity." It went abroad as "plasticity." They began to call it, as I myself often did then, "the third dimension." It was only a single phase of "continuity" but a phase that has come back home again to go to work on the surface and upon the novice. It will do him no harm as it is. But were the full import of continuity in architecture to be grasped, aesthetic and structure become completely one, it would continue to revolutionize the use and wont of our machine age architecture, making it superior in harmony and beauty to any architecture, Gothic or Greek. This ideal at work upon materials by nature of the process or tools used means a living architecture in a new age, organic architecture, the only architecture that can live and let live because it never can become a mere style. Nor can it ever become a formula for the tyro. Where principle is put to work, not as recipe or as formula, there will always be *style* and no need to bury it as "a style."

Although the wrap-around window, originally a minor outward expression of the interior folded plane in my own buildings, and various other minor features of the work of this period intended to simplify and eliminate "parts" are now scattered around the world and have become the rather senseless features of various attempts at formula, such as the sporadic "international" and other attempts characterized by plain surfaces cut into patterns by simple large openings, nevertheless the ideas behind these earlier appearances, the fundamental ideas that made them genuine expressions of architecture, have been altogether missed. The nature of materials is ignored in these imitations to get block mass outlines. The reverse of the period wherein mass material outlines tried to ignore the materials. But it is the same mistake.

The word "plastic" was a word Louis Sullivan himself was fond of using in reference to his scheme of ornamentation as distinguished from all other or any *applied* ornament. But now, and not merely as "form following function," came a larger application of the element called plasticity. "Form follows function" is mere dogma until you realize the higher truth that form and function are one.

Why any principle working in the part if not working in the whole?

I promoted plasticity as conceived by Lieber Meister to *continuity* in the concept of the building as a whole. If the dictum, "form follows function," had any bearing at all on building it could take form in architecture only by means of plasticity when seen at work as complete *continuity*. So why not throw away entirely all implications of post and beam construction? Have no posts, no columns, no pilasters, cornices or moldings or ornament; no divisions of the sort nor allow any fixtures whatever to enter as something added to the structure. Any building should be complete, including all within itself. Instead of many things, *one* thing.

The folded plane enters here with the merging lines, walls and ceilings made one. Let walls, ceilings, floors now become not only party to each other but *part of each other,* reacting upon and within one another; continuity in all, eliminating any merely constructed features as such, or any fixture or appliance whatsoever as such.

When Louis Sullivan had eliminated background in his system of ornament in favor of an integral sense of the whole he had implied this larger sense of the thing. I now began to achieve it.

Conceive that here came a new sense of building on American soil that could *grow* building forms not only true to function but expressive far beyond mere function in the realm of the human spirit. Our new country might now have a true architecture hitherto unknown. Yes, architectural forms by this interior means might now grow up to express a deeper sense of human life values than any existing before. Architecture might extend the bounds of human individuality indefinitely by way of safe interior discipline. Not only had space come upon a new technique of its own but every material and every method might now speak for itself in objective terms of human life. Architects were no longer tied to Greek space but were free to enter into the space of Einstein.

Architectural forms might *grow* up? Yes, but grow up in what image? Here came concentrated appeal to pure imagination. Gradually proceeding from generals to particulars in the field of work with materials and machines, "plasticity" (become "continuity") began to grip me and work its own will in architecture. I would watch sequences fascinated, seeing other sequences in those consequences already in evidence. I occasionally look through such early studies as I made at this period (a number of them still remain), fascinated by implications. They seem, even now, generic. The old architecture, always dead for me so far as its grammar went, began literally to disappear. As if by magic new effects came to life as though by themselves and I could draw inspiration from nature herself. I was beholden to no man for the look of anything. Textbook for me? "The book of creation." No longer need any more to be a wanderer among the objects and traditions of the past, picking and choosing his way by the personal idiosyncrasy of taste, guided only by personal predilection. From this hell I had been saved. The world lost an eclectic and gained an interpreter. If I did not like the Gods now I could make better ones.

Visions of simplicities so broad and far reaching would open to me and such building harmonies appear that I was tireless in search of new ones. In various form researches, with all my energy I concentrated upon the principle of plasticity working as continuity. Soon a practical working technique evolved and a new scale within the buildings I was building in the endeavor to more sensibly and sensitively accomplish this thing we call architecture. Here at work was something that would change and deepen the thinking and culture of the modern world. So I believed. . . .

From some laboratory experiments at Princeton by Professor Beggs which I saw while there delivering the Kahn Lectures in 1930, it appears that aesthetic "continuity" at work in the practice of physical structure is concrete proof of the practical usefulness of the aesthetic ideal in designing architectural forms and, I hope, may soon be available as structural formula in some handbook. Welding instead of riveting steel is one new means to this new end and other plastic methods are constantly coming into use. But that and other possibilities (they will, I hope and believe, never need) are ahead of our story.

There were then no symbols at all for these ideas. But I have already objectified most of them. Were architecture bricks, my hands were in the mud of which bricks were made.

An idea soon came from this stimulating simplifying ideal

(ideas breed, especially in actually making them work) that in order to be consistent, or indeed if all were to be put to work as architecture successfully, this new element of plasticity should have a new *sense* as well as a new *science* of materials.

It may interest you to know (it surprised me) that there is nothing in the literature of the civilized world upon that subject. Nothing I could find as *interpretation* in this sense of the nature of materials. Here was another great field for concrete endeavor, neglected. So I began, in my fashion, to study the nature of materials. Life is short. Lieber Meister had not reached this study. All materials alike were to receive the impress of his imagination. I began to learn to see brick as brick. I learned to see wood as wood and learned to see concrete or glass or metal each for itself and all as themselves. Strange to say this required uncommon sustained concentration of uncommon imagination (we call it vision), demanded not only a new conscious approach to building but opened a new world of thought that would certainly tear down the old world completely. Each different material required a different handling, and each different handling as well as the material itself had new possibilities of use peculiar to the nature of each. Appropriate designs for one material would not be at all appropriate for any other material. In the light of this ideal of building form as an organic simplicity almost all architecture fell to the ground. That is to say, ancient buildings were obsolete in the light of the idea of space determining form from within, all materials modifying if indeed they did not create the "form" when used with understanding according to the limitations of process and purpose.

Architecture might, and did, begin life anew.

Had steel, concrete, and glass existed in the ancient order we could have had nothing like our ponderous, senseless "classic" architecture. No, nothing even at Washington. Such betrayal of new life and new opportunities as ours has been would have been impossible to the ancients, the Greeks excepted, and we should have had a practice of architecture by the eclectic wherein tradition was not a parasite nor an enemy but a friend because the ancestors would have done the necessary work for us that we seem unable to do for ourselves. We would then have been able to copy the antique with sense and safety. Myself with the others.

Now there can be no organic architecture where the nature of synthetic materials or the nature of nature materials either is ignored or misunderstood. How can there be? Perfect correlation, integration, is life. It is the first principle of any growth that the thing grown be no mere aggregation. Integration as entity is first essential. And integration means that no part of anything is of any great value in itself except as it be integrate part of the harmonious whole. Even my great old master designed for materials all alike. All were grist for his rich imagination and he lived completely as artist, all to the contrary notwithstanding, only with his sentient ornament. Contrary to the ideas formed of him by word-wise but superficial critics, in this he created out of himself a world of his own, not yet appreciated at its true worth. How could it be yet? In this expression he went beyond the capacities of any individual before him. But all materials were only one material to him in which to weave the stuff of his dreams. Terra cotta was that one material. Terra cotta was *his* material, the one he loved most and served best. There he was master. But I honored him when I carried his work and thought further along by acting upon this new train of ideas, and the acts soon brought work sharply and immediately up against the tools that could be found to get these ideas put into new forms of building.

What a man does—*that* he has. You may find other things on him but they are not his.

What were the tools in use in the building trades everywhere? *Machines* and the automatic process, all too many of them. Stone or wood planers, stone and wood molding shapers, various lathes, presses, and power saws, the casting of metals and glass; all in commercially organized mills. The kiln; sheet-metal breakers; presses; shears; cutting, molding, and stamping machines in foundries and rolling mills; commercialized machine "shops"; concrete mixers; clay breakers; casters; glassmakers themselves; and the trade-unions versus capital; all laborers' or employers' units in a more or less highly commercialized greater union in which craftsmanship had no place except as survival for burial by standardization. Quantity production or standardization was already inflexible necessity either as enemy or friend. You might choose. And as you chose you became master and useful, or a luxury and eventually the more or less elegant parasite we call an "eclectic"; a man guided only by instinct of choice called "taste."

By now I did not choose by instinct. I felt, yes, but I *knew* now what it was I felt concerning architecture.

Already, when I began to build, commercial machine standardization had taken the life of handicraft. But outworn handicraft had never troubled me. To make the new forms living expression of the new order of the machine and continue what was noble in tradition did trouble me. I wanted to realize genuine new forms true to the spirit of great tradition and found I should have to make them; not only make forms appropriate to the old (natural) and to new (synthetic) materials, but I should have to so design them that the machine (or process) that must make them could and would make them better than anything could possibly be made by hand. But now with this sense of integral order in architecture supreme in my mind I could have done nothing less unless I could have commanded armies of craftsmen as later I did command them in the building of the Imperial Hotel: a building in no sense a product of machine method. By now, safe inner discipline had come to me: the interior discipline of a great ideal. There is none so severe. But no other discipline yields such rich rewards in work, nor is there any man so safe and sure of results as the man disciplined from within by this ideal of the integration that is organic. Experience is this man's "school." It is yet his only school.

As I put these ideas to work in materials, lesser ideas took flight from this exacting ideal. But always in the same direction. They went farther on each occasion for flight, which was each new building I built, until great goals were in sight. Some few of the goals have been partially realized. You may see the "signs and portents" gathered together in various exhibition galleries if you can read drawings and models. The photographs are poor because the depth planes cannot be rendered by photography. But a number of the buildings are scattered or mutilated and unfortunately most of the best drawings are gone. The best buildings, too, were never built and may only be studied by the record. But later designs and models all exemplify in some material or grouping of materials, or idea of arrangement, these early objectives. Lieber Meister had been searching for "the rule so broad as to admit of no exception." For the life of me I could not help being most interested in the exception that proved the rule. This may explain "inconsistency" in performance and apparent departure from original objectives.

A group of young Chicago architects were gathered about me as disciples and friends in the early days, about 1893. They were my contemporaries and all learned from me to speak the new language. I wrote a little and later I tried to stem the tide of imitation. An instance was the paper read at Hull House in 1904 on "The Art and Craft of the Machine." Occasionally, then an indifferent lecturer, I lectured. But talking isn't building, as I soon saw where any "school" as they called it (and later had names for the branches) had actually *to build*. Among these contemporaries the more ambitious began to call the new dwellings that appeared upon the prairies from 1893 to 1910 "the prairie school." I suppose this was modern architecture's first gallery. None knew much of Louis Sullivan, then, except by such work as he had done. And to a certain extent they imitated him too; imitating his individual ornamentation as the feature most in view. Some years later C. R. Ashbee came over to the United States and Kuno Francke of Harvard came to Oak Park. Both, in turn, saw the new work on the prairies and carried the tale of it to Europe in 1908. Some 15 or 20 years later a Swiss (in France) was to rediscover a familiar preliminary aesthetic; the affirmative negation declared by the Larkin Building, widely published at the time when it was built and recorded by an article in the *Architectural Record*, March 1908. But already (1910) in my own work the ideal of an organic architecture as affirmation had gone far beyond that belated negation that was at work in Europe itself.

Before trying to put down more in detail concerning goals now in sight, popular reaction to this new endeavor might be interesting. After the first "prairie house" was built, the Winslow house in 1893, which only in the matter of ornamentation bore resemblance in respect to the master (in the Charnley house I had stated, for the first time so far as I know, the thesis of the plain wall given the nature of decoration by a well-placed single opening which is also a feature of the Winslow house), my next client said he did not want a house "so different that he would have to go down the back way to his morning train to avoid being laughed at." That was one popular consequence. There were many others; bankers at first refused to loan money on the "queer" houses, so friends had to be found to finance the early buildings. Millmen would soon look for the name on the plans when the plans were presented for estimates, read the name of the architect and roll up the drawings again, handing them back with the remark that "they were not hunting for trouble"; contractors more often than not failed to read the plans correctly, so much had to be left off the buildings. The buildings were already off the main track. The clients themselves usually stood by interested and excited, often way beyond their means. So, when they moved into their new house, quite frequently they had no money left, had borrowed all they could and had to drag their old furniture into their new world. Seldom could I complete an interior because the ideal of "organic simplicity" seen as the countenance of perfect integration (as you have already read) naturally abolished all fixtures, rejected the old furniture, all carpets and most hangings, declaring them to be irrelevant or superficial decoration. The new practice made all furnishings so far as possible (certainly the electric lighting and heating systems) integral parts of the architecture. So far as possible all furniture was to be designed in place as part of the building. Hangings, rugs, carpets, were they to be used (as they might be if properly designed), all came into the same category. But the money matter generally crippled this particular feature of the original scheme, as I have said, and made trouble in this process of elimination and integration.

Nor, theoretically, was any planting to be done about the houses without cooperating with the architect. But, of course, it was done more often than not. But no sculpture, no painting was let in unless cooperating with the architect, although more often than not pictures were "hung." This made trouble. For no decoration, as such, was to be seen anywhere. Sculpture and painting were to be likewise *of* the building itself. In the Midway Gardens built in Chicago in 1913 I tried to complete the synthesis: planting, furnishings, music, painting, and sculpture, all to be one. But I found musicians, painters, and sculptors were unable to rise at that time to any such synthesis. Only in a grudging and dim way did most of them even understand it as an idea. So I made the designs for all to harmonize with the architecture; crude as any sketch is crude, incomplete as to execution, but in effect sufficiently complete to show the immense importance of any such attempt on any architect's part and show, indeed, that only so does architecture completely live. A new ideal of ornamentation had by now arrived that wiped out all ornament unless it, too, was an integral feature of the whole. True ornament became more desirable than ever but it had to "mean something"; in other words *be* something organic in character. Decorators hunting a job would visit the owners and, learning the name of the architect, lift their hats, turn on their heels, leaving with the curt and sarcastic "good day!" meaning really what the slang "good night!" of the period meant. This matter of integral ornament is the rock upon which a later generation of young architects splits and wisely decides to let it alone for the time being.

The owners of the early houses were, of course, all subjected to curiosity, sometimes to admiration, but were submitted most often to the ridicule of the "middle of the road egotist." To that ubiquitous egotist there was something about the owner too, now, when he had a house like that, "the rope tie around the monkey's neck."

Well, I soon had to face the fact that a different choice of materials would mean a different building altogether. Concrete was just coming into use and Unity Temple became the first concrete monolith in the world, that is to say, the first building complete as monolithic architecture when the wooden forms in which it was cast were taken away. No critic has yet seen it as it is for what it is except to realize that here, at least, was *something*. They might not like the temple but they were "impressed" by it. Meanwhile, the Larkin Building at Buffalo had just been built, a consciously important challenge to the empty ornamentality of the old order. The phrases I myself used concerning it in the issue of the *Architectural Record* in 1908 devoted to my work, put it on record as such. "Here again most of the critic's architecture has been left out. Therefore, the work may have the same claim to consideration as a work of art, as an ocean liner, a locomotive, or a battleship." The words may have escaped the Swiss "discoverer"; he was young at the time.

Plastered houses were then new. Casement windows were new. So many things were new. Nearly everything was new but the law of gravity and the idiosyncrasy of the client.

And simple as the buildings seemed and seem to be to this day because all had character and the countenance of principle, only the outward countenance of their simplicity has ever taken effect and that countenance is now being variously exaggerated by confirmed eclectics for the sake of the effect of a style. The innate simplicity that enabled them and enables them to multiply in infinite variety has not been practiced. I had built 187 buildings, planned and detailed about 37 more that had not been built, and all together they did not classify as a style. Nevertheless, all had "style."

As reward for independent thinking put into action as building and first plainly shown in the constitution and profiles of the prairie houses of Oak Park, Riverside, and other suburbs and Chicago and other cities, Unity Temple at Oak Park and the Larkin Administration Building in Buffalo, an entirely new sense of architecture for anyone who could read architecture had emerged. A higher concept of architecture. Architecture not alone as "form following function" in Lieber Meister's sense but architecture for the spirit of man, for life as life must be lived today; architecture spiritually (virtually) conceived as appropriate enclosure of interior space to be lived in. Form and function made one. The enclosed space within them is the *reality* of the building. The enclosed space comes through as architecture and may be seen in these exteriors I have built as the *reality* of the building I wanted to build and did build and am still building in spite of all opposition and the supreme obstacle, pretentious ignorance. This sense of the "within" or the room itself (or the rooms themselves) I see as the great thing to be realized and that may take the new forms we need as architecture. Such a source would never stultify itself as a mere style. This sense of interior space made *exterior* as architecture, working out by way of the nature of materials and tools, transcends, as a fertilizing motive, all that has ever gone before in architecture. This clarifying motive of the whole makes previous ideas useful only as a means to the realization of this far greater concept of architecture. But if the buildings I have conceived upon this basis still seem enigmatical, most of all they must seem so to those who profess the "modernistic." A chasm exists between the usual professsion and performance, because growth, where the quality we now call organic is concerned, must be slow growth. Eclecticism may take place overnight but organic architecture must come from the ground up into the light by gradual growth. It will itself be the ground of a better way of life; it is not only the beautifier of the building; it is, as a circumstance in itself, becoming the blessing of the occupants. All building construction naturally becomes lighter and stronger as fibrous "integument" takes the place of "solid mass." Our arboreal ancestors in their trees seem more likely precedent for us at the present time than savage animals who "hole in" for protection. But to properly put it on a human level, a higher *order* of the spirit has dawned for modern life in this interior concept of lived-in space playing with light, taking organic form as the reality of building; a building now an entity by way of native materials and natural methods of structure; forms becoming more naturally significant of ideal and purpose, ultimate in economy and strength. We have, now coming clear, an ideal the core of which must soon pervade the whole realm of creative man and one that, I know now, dates back to Laotse 500 B.C., and, later, to Jesus himself. The building era that Louis Sullivan ushered in is developing beyond the limitations that marked it, aside from his splendid elemental fluorescence, into the higher realm where as a human creative ideal throughout all culture it will make all form and function one.

Not much yet exists in our country—no, nor in any country outside plans and models—to exemplify steel and glass at its best in the light of this new sense of building. But a new countenance —it is the countenance of principle—has already appeared around the world. A new architectural language is being brokenly, variously, and often falsely spoken by youths, with perspicacity and some breadth of view but with too little depth of knowledge that can only come from continued experience. Unfortunately, academic training and current criticism have no penetration to this inner world. The old academic order is bulging with its own important impotence. Society is cracking under the strain of a sterility education imposes far beyond capacity; exaggerated capitalism has left all this as academic heritage to its own youth. General cultural sterility, the cause of the unrest of this uncreative moment that now stalls the world, might be saved and fructified by this ideal of an organic architecture: led from shallow troubled muddy water into deeper clearer pools of thought. Life needs these deeper fresher pools into which youth may plunge to come out refreshed.

More and more, so it seems to me, light is the beautifier of the building. Light always was the beautifier of the building in the matter of shadows but now especially needs these deeper satisfactions; needs a more worthy human ego for that tomorrow that is always today because of yesterday.

Inevitably this deeper sense of building as integral produce of the spirit of man is to construct the physical body of our machine age. But that in itself will not be enough. Unless this construction were to enable a broader, finer sense of life as something to be lived in to the full, all resources of time, place, and man in place to give us an architecture that is inspiring environment at the same time that it is a true expression of that life itself, the ideal will again have failed.

These gestures being lightly called "modernistic," what then is this new lip service, in shops, studios and schoolrooms? What are these pretentious gestures, this superficial association of ideas or this attempted academic rationalizing of this new work of mine? Why is the true content or motivating inner thought of this new architecture as organic architecture so confused in their hypocritical manifestations? Why is there so little modest, earnest effort to profit honestly by cooperation in these researches and, understanding such proofs as we have, honestly use them, such as they are?

Why not go ahead with them for growth instead of continuing to exploit them for a living or for a passing name? This self-seeking of some transient fame? "Publicity" is the only fame such shallow ambition may know, and like all such ambitions only the "advertising" that will be dead with yesterday's newspaper.

BUILDING THE NEW HOUSE

First thing in building the new house, get rid of the attic, therefore the dormer. Get rid of the useless false heights below it. Next, get rid of the unwholesome basement, yes absolutely—in any house built on the prairie. Instead of lean, brick chimneys bristling up everywhere to hint at Judgment, I could see necessity for one chimney only. A broad generous one, or at most two. These kept low down on gently sloping roofs or perhaps flat roofs. The big fireplace in the house below became now a place for a real fire. A real fireplace at that time was extraordinary. There were mantels instead. A mantel was a marble frame for a few coals in a grate. Or it was a piece of wooden furniture with tile stuck in it around the grate, the whole set slam up against the plastered, papered wall. Insult to comfort. So the *integral* fireplace became an important part of the building itself in the houses I was allowed to build out there on the prairie.

It comforted me to see the fire burning deep in the solid masonry of the house itself. A feeling that came to stay.

Taking a human being for my scale, I brought the whole house down in height to fit a normal one—ergo, 5′ 8½″ tall, say. This is my own height. Believing in no other scale than the human being I broadened the mass out all I possibly could to bring it down into spaciousness. It has been said that were I three inches taller than 5′ 8½″ all my houses would have been quite different in proportion. Probably.

House walls were now started at the ground on a cement or stone water table that looked like a low platform under the building, and usually was. But the house walls were stopped at the second-story windowsill level to let the bedrooms come through above in a continuous window series below the broad eaves of a gently sloping, overhanging roof. In this new house the wall was beginning to go as an impediment to outside light and air and beauty. Walls had been the great fact about the box in which holes had to be punched. It was still this conception of a wall-building which was with me when I designed the Winslow house. But after that my conception began to change.

My sense of "wall" was no longer the side of a box. It was enclosure of space affording protection against storm or heat only when needed. But it was also to bring the outside world into the house and let the inside of the house go outside. In this sense I was working away at the wall as a wall and bringing it towards the function of a screen, a means of opening up space which, as control of building-materials improved, would finally permit the free use of the whole space without affecting the soundness of the structure. ●

The climate being what it was, violent in extremes of heat and cold, damp and dry, dark and bright, I gave broad protecting roof-shelter to the whole, getting back to the purpose for which the cornice was originally designed. The underside of roof-projections was flat and usually light in color to create a glow of reflected light that softly brightened the upper rooms. Overhangs had double value: shelter and preservation for the walls of the house, as well as this diffusion of reflected light for the upper story through the "light screens" that took the place of the walls and were now often the windows in long series.

And at this time I saw a house, primarily, as livable interior space under ample shelter. I liked the *sense of shelter* in the look of the building. I still like it.

The house began to associate with the ground and become natural to its prairie site.

And would the young man in Architecture believe that this was all "new" then? Yes—not only new, but destructive heresy—ridiculous eccentricity. All somewhat so today. Stranger still, but then it was *all* so *new* that what prospect I had of ever earning a livelihood by making houses was nearly wrecked. At first, "they" called the houses "dress reform" houses because Society was just then excited about that particular reform. This simplification looked like some kind of reform to the provincials.

What I have just described was on the *outside* of the house. But it was all there, chiefly because of what had happened *inside*.

Dwellings of that period were cut up, advisedly and completely, with the grim determination that should go with any cutting process. The interiors consisted of boxes beside boxes or inside boxes, called *rooms*. All boxes were inside a complicated outside boxing. Each domestic function was properly box to box.

I could see little sense in this inhibition, this cellular sequestration that implied ancestors familiar with penal institutions, except for the privacy of bedrooms on the upper floor. They were perhaps all right as sleeping boxes. So I declared the whole lower floor as one room, cutting off the kitchen as a laboratory, putting the servants' sleeping and living quarters next to the kitchen but semi-detached, on the ground floor. Then I screened various portions of the big room for certain domestic purposes like dining and reading.

There were no plans in existence like these at the time. But my clients were all pushed toward these ideas as helpful to a solution of the vexed servant problem. Scores of unnecessary doors disappeared and no end of partition. Both clients and servants liked the new freedom. The house became more free as space and more livable too. Interior spaciousness began to dawn.

Thus came an end to the cluttered house. Fewer doors; fewer window holes though much greater window area; windows and doors lowered to convenient human heights. These changes once made, the ceilings of the rooms could be brought down over on to the walls by way of the horizontal broad bands of plaster on the walls themselves above the windows and colored the same as the room-ceilings. This would bring ceiling-surface and color down to the very window tops. Ceilings thus expanded by way of the wall band above the windows gave generous overhead even to small rooms. The sense of the whole broadened, made plastic by this means.

Here entered the important new element of plasticity—as I saw it. And I saw it as indispensable element to the successful use of the machine. The windows would sometimes be wrapped around the building corners as inside emphasis of plasticity and to increase the sense of interior space. I fought for outswinging windows because the casement window associated house with the out-of-doors, gave free openings outward. In other words, the so-called casement was not only simple but more human in use and effect. So more natural. If it had not existed I should have invented it. But it was not used at that time in the United States so I lost many clients because I insisted upon it. The client usually wanted the double-hung (the guillotine window) in use then, although it was neither simple nor human. It was only expedient. I used it once, in the Winslow house, and rejected it forever thereafter. Nor at that time did I entirely eliminate the wooden trim. I did make the "trim" plastic, that is to say, light and continuously flowing instead of the prevailing heavy "cut and butt" carpenter work. No longer did trim, so-called, look like carpenter work. The machine could do it all perfectly well as I laid it out, in this search for quiet. This plastic trim enabled poor workmanship to be concealed. There was need of that much trim then to conceal much in the way of craftsmanship because the battle between the machines and the union had already begun to demoralize workmen.

Machine resources of this period were so little understood that extensive drawings had to be made merely to show the mill-man what to leave off. Not alone in the trim but in numerous ways too tedious to describe in words, this revolutionary sense of the *plastic* whole began to work more and more intelligently and have fascinating unforeseen consequences. Nearly everyone had endured the house of the period as long as possible, judging by the appreciation of the change. Here was an ideal of organic simplicity put to work, with historical consequences not only in this country but especially in the thought of the civilized world.

SIMPLICITY

Organic Simplicity—in this early constructive effort—I soon found depended upon the sympathy with which such co-ordination as I have described might be effected. Plainness was not necessarily simplicity. That was evident. Crude furniture of the Roycroft-Stickley-Mission style, which came along later, was offensively plain, plain as a barn door—but was never simple in any true sense. Nor, I found, were merely machine-made things in themselves necessarily simple. "To think," as the Master used to say, "is to deal in simples." And that means with an eye single to the altogether.

This is, I believe, the single secret of simplicity: that we may truly regard nothing at all as simple in itself. I believe that no one thing in itself is ever so, but must achieve simplicity—as an artist should use the term—as a perfectly realized part of some organic whole. Only as a feature or any part becomes harmonious element in the harmonious whole does it arrive at the state of simplicity. Any wild flower is truly simple but double the same wild flower by cultivation and it ceases to be so. The scheme of the original is no longer clear. Clarity of design and perfect significance both are first essentials of the spontaneous born simplicity of the lilies of the field. "They toil not, neither do they spin." Jesus wrote the supreme essay on simplicity in this, "Consider the lilies of the field."

Five lines where three are enough is always stupidity. Nine pounds where three are sufficient is obesity. But to eliminate expressive words in speaking or writing—words that intensify or vivify meaning—is not simplicity. Nor is similar elimination in architecture simplicity. It may be, and usually is, stupidity.

In architecture, expressive changes of surface, emphasis of line and especially textures of material or imaginative pattern, may go to make facts more eloquent—forms more significant. Elimination, therefore, may be just as meaningless as elaboration, perhaps more often is so. To know what to leave out and what to put in; just where and just how, ah, *that* is to have been educated in knowledge of simplicity—toward ultimate freedom of expression.

As for objects of art in the house, even in that early day they were bêtes noires of the new simplicity. If well chosen, all right.

But only if each were properly digested by the whole. Antique or modern sculpture, paintings, pottery, might well enough become objectives in the architectural scheme. And I accepted them, aimed at them often but assimilated them. Such precious things may often take their places as elements in the design of any house, be gracious and good to live with. But such assimilation is extraordinarily difficult. Better in general to design all as integral features.

I tried to make my clients see that furniture and furnishings that were not built in as integral features of the building should be designed as attributes of whatever furniture *was* built in and should be seen as a minor part of the building itself even if detached or kept aside to be employed only on occasion.

But when the building itself was finished the old furniture they already possessed usually went in with the clients to await the time when the interior might be completed in this sense. Very few of the houses, therefore, were anything but painful to me after the clients brought in their belongings.

Soon I found it difficult, anyway, to make some of the furniture in the abstract. That is, to design it as architecture and make it human at the same time—fit for human use. I have been black and blue in some spot, somewhere, almost all my life from too intimate contact with my own early furniture.

Human beings must group, sit or recline, confound them, and they must dine—but dining is much easier to manage and always a great artistic opportunity. Arrangements for the informality of sitting in comfort singly or in groups still belonging in disarray to the scheme as a whole: *that* is a matter difficult to accomplish. But it can be done now and should be done, because only those attributes of human comfort and convenience should be in order which belong to the whole in this modern integrated sense.

Human use and comfort should not be taxed to pay dividends on any designer's idiosyncrasy. Human use and comfort should have intimate possession of every interior—should be felt in every exterior. Decoration is intended to make use more charming and comfort more appropriate, or else a privilege has been abused.

As these ideals worked away from house to house, finally freedom of floor space and elimination of useless heights worked a miracle in the new dwelling place. A sense of appropriate freedom had changed its whole aspect. The whole became different but more fit for human habitation and more natural on its site. It was impossible to imagine a house once built on these principles somewhere else. An entirely new sense of space-values in architecture came home. It now appears these new values came into the architecture of the world. New sense of repose in quiet streamline effects had arrived. The streamline and the plain surface seen as the flat plane had then and there, some thirty-seven years ago, found their way into buildings as we see them in steamships, aeroplanes and motorcars, although they were intimately related to building materials, environment and the human being.

But, more important than all beside, still rising to greater dignity as an idea as it goes on working, was the ideal of plasticity. That ideal now began to emerge as a means to achieve an organic architecture.

PLASTICITY

Plasticity may be seen in the expressive flesh-covering of the skeleton as contrasted with the articulation of the skeleton itself. If form really "followed function"—as the Master declared—here was the direct means of expression of the more spiritual idea that form and function are one: the only true means I could see then or can see now to eliminate the separation and complication of cut-and-butt joinery in favor of the expressive flow of continuous surface. Here, by instinct at first—all ideas germinate—a principle entered into building that has since gone on developing. In my work the idea of plasticity may now be seen as the element of continuity.

In architecture, plasticity is only the modern expression of an ancient thought. But the thought taken into structure and throughout human affairs will re-create in a badly "disjointed," distracted world the entire fabric of human society. This magic word "plastic" was a word Louis Sullivan himself was fond of using in reference to his idea of ornamentation as distinguished from all other or applied ornament. But now, why not the larger application in the structure of the building itself in this sense?

Why a principle working in the part if not living in the whole?

If form really followed function—it did in a material sense by means of this ideal of plasticity, the spiritual concept of *form and function as one*—why not throw away the implications of post or upright and beam or horizontal entirely? Have no beams or columns piling up as "joinery." Nor any cornices. Nor any "features" as *fixtures*. No. Have no appliances of any kind at all, such as pilasters, entablatures and cornices. Nor put into the building any fixtures whatsoever as "fixtures." Eliminate the separations and separate joints. Classic architecture was all fixation-of-the-fixture. Yes, entirely so. Now why not let walls, ceilings, floors become *seen* as component parts of each other, their surfaces flowing into each other. To get continuity in the whole, eliminating all constructed features just as Louis Sullivan had eliminated background in his ornament in favor of an integral sense of the whole. Here the promotion of an idea from the material to the spiritual plane began to have consequences. Conceive now that an entire building might grow up out of conditions as a plant grows up out of soil and yet be free to be itself, to "live its own life according to Man's Nature." Dignified as a tree in the midst of nature but a child of the spirit of man.

I now propose an ideal for the architecture of the machine age, for the ideal American building. Let it grow up in that image. The tree.

But I do not mean to suggest the imitation of the tree.

Proceeding, then, step by step from generals to particulars, plasticity as a large means in architecture began to grip me and to work its own will. Fascinated I would watch its sequences, seeing other sequences in those consequences already in evidence: as in the Heurtley, Martin, Heath, Thomas, Tomek, Coonley and dozens of other houses.

The old architecture, so far as its grammar went, for me began, literally, to disappear. As if by magic new architectural effects came to life—effects genuinely new in the whole cycle of architecture owing simply to the working of this spiritual principle. Vistas of inevitable simplicity and ineffable harmonies would open, so beautiful to me that I was not only delighted, but often startled. Yes, sometimes amazed.

I have since concentrated on plasticity as physical continuity, using it as a practical working principle within the very nature of the building itself in the effort to accomplish this great thing called architecture. Every true esthetic is an implication of nature, so it was inevitable that this esthetic ideal should be found to enter into the actual building of the building itself as a principle of construction.

But later on I found that in the effort to actually eliminate the post and beam in favor of structural continuity, that is to say, making the two things one thing instead of two separate things, I could get no help at all from regular engineers. By habit, the engineer reduced everything in the field of calculation to the post and the beam resting upon it before he could calculate and tell you where and just how much for either. He had no other data. Walls made one with floors and ceilings, merging together yet reacting upon each other, the engineer had never met. And the engineer has not yet enough scientific formulae to enable him to calculate for continuity. Floor slabs stiffened and extended as cantilevers over centered supports, as a waiter's tray rests upon his upturned fingers, such as I now began to use in order to get planes parallel to the earth to emphasize the third dimension, were new, as I used them, especially in the Imperial Hotel. But the engineer soon mastered the element of continuity in floor slabs, with such formulae as he had. The cantilever thus became a new feature of design in architecture. As used in the Imperial Hotel at Tokyo it was the most important of the features of construction that insured the life of that building in the terrific temblor of 1922. So, not only a new esthetic but proving the esthetic as scientifically sound, a great new economic "stability," derived from steel in tension, was able now to enter into building construction.

IN THE NATURE OF MATERIALS:

A PHILOSOPHY

Our vast resources are yet new; new only because architecture as "rebirth" (perennial Renaissance) has, after five centuries of decline, culminated in the imitation of imitations, seen in our Mrs. Plaster-built, Mrs. Gablemore, and Miss Flat-top American architecture. In general, and especially officially, our architecture is at long last completely significant of insignificance only. We do not longer have architecture. At least no buildings with integrity. We have only economic crimes in its name. No, our greatest buildings are not qualified as great art, my dear Mrs. Davies, although you do admire Washington.

If you will yet be patient for a little while—a scientist, Einstein, asked for three days to explain the far less pressing and practical matter of "Relativity"—we will take each of the five new resources in order, as with the five fingers of the hand. All are new integrities to be used if we will to make living easier and better today.

The first great integrity is a deeper, more intimate sense of reality in building than was ever pagan—that is to say, than was ever "Classic." More human than was any building ever realized in the Christian Middle Ages. This is true although the thought that may ennoble it now has been living in civilization for more than twenty centuries back. Later it was innate in the simplicities of Jesus as it was organic 500 years earlier in the natural philosophy, Tao (The Way), of the Chinese philosopher Laotse. But not only is the new architecture sound philosophy. It is poetry.

Said Ong Giao Ki, Chinese sage, "Poetry is the sound of the heart."

Well, like poetry, this sense of architecture is the sound of the "within." We might call that "within," the heart.

Architecture now becomes integral, the expression of a new-old reality: the livable interior space of the room itself. In integral architecture the *room-space itself must come through.* The *room* must be seen as architecture, or we have no architecture. We have no longer an outside as outside. We have no longer an outside and an inside as two separate things. Now the outside may come inside, and the inside may and does go outside. They are *of* each other. Form and function thus become one in design and execution if the nature of materials and method and purpose are all in unison.

This interior-space concept, the first broad integrity, is the first great resource. It is also true basis for general significance of form. Add to this for the sake of clarity that (although the general integration is implied in the first integrity) it is in the nature of any organic building to grow from its site, come out of the ground into the light—the ground itself held always as a component basic part of the building itself. And then we have primarily the new ideal of building as organic. A building dignified as a tree in the midst of nature.

This new ideal for architecture is, as well, an adequate ideal for our general culture. In any final result there can be no separation between our architecture and our culture. Nor any separation of either from our happiness. Nor any separation from our work.

Thus in this rise of organic integration you see the means to end the petty agglomerations miscalled civilization. By way of this old yet new and deeper sense of reality we may have a civilization. In this sense we now recognize and may declare by way of plan and building—the *natural.* Faith in the *natural* is the faith we now need to grow up on in this coming age of our culturally confused, backward twentieth century. But instead of "organic" we might well say "natural" building. Or we might say integral building.

So let us now consider the second of the five new resources: glass. This second resource is new and a "super-material" only because it holds such amazing means in modern life for awakened sensibilities. It amounts to a new qualification of life in itself. If known in ancient times glass would then and there have abolished the ancient architecture we know, and completely. This super-material GLASS as we now use it is a miracle. Air in air to keep air out or keep it in. Light itself in light, to diffuse or reflect, or refract light itself.

By means of glass, then, the first great integrity may find prime means of realization. Open reaches of the ground may enter as the building and the building interior may reach out and associate with these vistas of the ground. Ground and building will thus become more and more obvious as directly related to each other in openness and intimacy; not only as environment but also as a good pattern for the good life lived in the building. Realizing the benefits to human life of the far-reaching implications and effects of the first great integrity, let us call it the interior-space concept. This interior-space realization is possible and it is desirable in all the vast variety of characteristic buildings needed by civilized life in our complex age.

By means of glass something of the freedom of our arboreal ancestors living in their trees becomes a more likely precedent for freedom in twentieth-century life, than the cave.

Savage animals "holing in" for protection were more characteristic of life based upon the might of feudal times or based upon the so-called "classical" in architecture, which were in turn based upon the labor of the chattel slave. In a free country, were we ourselves free by way of organic thought, buildings might come out into the light without more animal fear; come entirely away from the pagan ideals of form we dote upon as "Classic." Or what Freedom have we?

Perhaps more important than all beside, it is by way of glass that the sunlit space as a reality becomes the most useful servant of a higher order of the human spirit. It is first aid to the sense of cleanliness of form and idea when directly related to free living in air and sunlight. It is this that is coming in the new architecture. And with the integral character of extended vistas gained by marrying buildings with ground levels, or blending them with slopes and gardens; yes, it is in this new sense of earth as a great human *good* that we will move forward in the building of our new homes and great public buildings.

I am certain we will desire the sun, spaciousness and integrity of means-to-ends more year by year as we become aware of the possibilities I have outlined. The more we desire the sun, the more we will desire the freedom of the good ground and the sooner we will learn to understand it. The more we value integrity, the more securely we will find and keep a worthwhile civilization to set against prevalent abuse and ruin.

Congestion will no longer encourage the "space-makers for

rent." The "space-maker for rent" will himself be "for rent" or let us hope "vacant." Give him ten years.

These new space values are entering into our ideas of life. All are appropriate to the ideal that is our own, the ideal we call Democracy.

A NEW REALITY: GLASS

A resource to liberate this new sense of interior space as reality is this new qualification called glass: a super-material qualified to qualify us; qualify us not only to escape from the prettified cavern of our present domestic life as also from the cave of our past, but competent actually to awaken in us the desire for such far-reaching simplicities of life as we may see in the clear countenance of nature. Good building must ever be seen as in the nature of good construction, but a higher development of this "seeing" will be construction seen as nature-pattern. *That* seeing, only, is inspired architecture.

This dawning sense of the *Within* as *reality* when it is clearly seen as *Nature* will by way of glass make the garden be the building as much as the building will be the garden: the sky as treasured a feature of daily indoor life as the ground itself.

You may see that walls are vanishing. The cave for human dwelling purposes is at last disappearing.

Walls themselves because of glass will become windows and windows as we used to know them as holes in walls will be seen no more. Ceilings will often become as window-walls, too. The textile may soon be used as a beautiful overhead for space, the textile an attribute of genuine architecture instead of decoration by way of hangings and upholstery. The usual camouflage of the old order. Modern integral floor heating will follow integral lighting and standardized unitary sanitation. All this makes it reasonable and good economy to abolish building as either a hyper-boxment or a super-borough.

Haven't senseless elaboration and false mass become sufficiently insulting and oppressive to our intelligence as a people? And yet, senseless elaboration and false mass were tyrannical as "conspicuous waste" in all of our nineteenth-century architecture either public or private! Wherever the American architect, as scholar, went he "succeeded" to that extent.

ANOTHER REALITY: CONTINUITY

But now, as third resource, the resource essential to modern architecture destined to cut down this outrageous mass-waste and mass-lying, is the principle of continuity. I have called it tenuity. Steel is its prophet and master. You must come with me for a moment into "engineering" so called. This is to be an unavoidable strain upon your kind attention. Because, unfortunately, gentle reader, you cannot understand architecture as *modern* unless you do come, and—paradox—you can't come if you are too well educated as an engineer or as an architect either. So your common sense is needed more than your erudition.

However, to begin this argument for steel: classic architecture knew only the post as an *upright*. Call it a column. The classics knew only the beam as a *horizontal*. Call it a beam. The beam resting upon the upright, or column, was structure throughout, to them. Two things, you see, one thing set on top of another thing in various materials and put there in various ways. Ancient, and nineteenth-century building science too, even building *à la mode*, consisted simply in reducing the various stresses of all materials and their uses to these two things: post and beam. Really, construction used to be just sticking up something in wood or stone and putting something else in wood or stone (maybe iron) on top of it: simple super-imposition, you see? You should know that all "Classic" architecture was and still is some such form of direct super-imposition. The arch is a little less so, but even that must be so "figured" by the structural engineer if you ask him to "figure" it.

Now the Greeks developed this simple act of super-imposition pretty far by way of innate tasteful refinement. The Greeks were true estheticians. Roman builders too, when they forgot the Greeks and brought the beam over as a curve by way of the arch, did something somewhat new but with consequences still of the same sort. But observe, all architectural features made by such "Classic" agglomeration were killed for us by cold steel. And though millions of classic corpses yet encumber American ground unburied, they are ready now for burial.

Of course this primitive post-and-beam construction will always be valid, but both support and supported may now by means of inserted and welded steel strands or especially woven filaments of steel and modern concrete casting be plaited and united as one physical body: ceilings and walls made one with floors and reinforcing each other by making them continue into one another. This Continuity is made possible by the tenuity of steel.

So the new order wherever steel or plastics enter construction says: weld these two things, post and beam (wall and ceiling) together by means of steel strands buried and stressed within the mass material itself, the steel strands electric-welded where steel meets steel within the mass. In other words the upright and horizontal may now be made to work together as one. A new world of form opens inevitably.

Where the beam leaves off and the post begins is no longer important nor need it be seen at all because it no longer actually *is*. Steel in tension enables the support to slide into the supported, or the supported to grow into the support somewhat as a tree-branch glides out of its tree trunk. Therefrom arises the new series of interior physical reactions I am calling "Continuity." As natural consequence the new esthetic or appearance we call *Plasticity* (and plasticity is peculiarly "modern") is no longer a mere appearance. Plasticity actually becomes the normal *countenance,* the *true esthetic* of genuine structural reality. These interwoven steel strands may so lie in so many directions in any extended member that the extensions may all be economical of material and though much lighter, be safer construction than ever before. There as in the branch of the tree you may see the cantilever. The cantilever is the simplest one of the important phases of this third new structural resource now demanding new significance. It has yet had little attention in architecture. It can do remarkable things to liberate space.

But plasticity was modest new countenance in our American architecture at least thirty-five years ago in my own work, but then denied such simple means as welding and the mesh. It had already eliminated all the separate identities of post and beam in architecture. Steel in tension enters now by way of mesh and welding to arrive at actual, total plasticity if and when desired by the architect. And to prove the philosophy of organic architecture, form and function are one, it now enters architecture as the *esthetic* countenance of *physical reality.*

To further illustrate this magic simplifier we call "plasticity": see it as *flexibility* similar to that of your own hand. What makes your hand expressive? Flowing continuous line and continuous surfaces seen continually mobile of the articulate articulated structure of the hand as a whole. The line is seen as "hand" line. The varying planes seen as "hand" surface. Strip the hand to the separate structural identities of joined bones (post and beam) and plasticity as an expression of the hand would disappear. We would be then getting back to the joinings, breaks, jolts, and joints of ancient, or "Classic," architecture: thing to thing; feature to feature. But plasticity is the reverse of that ancient agglomeration and is the ideal means behind these simplified free new effects of straight line and flat plane.

I have just said that plasticity in this sense for thirty-five years or more has been the recognized esthetic ideal for such simplification as was required by the machine to do organic work. And it is true of my own work.

As significant outline and expressive surface, this new esthetic of plasticity (physical continuity) is now a useful means to form the supreme physical body of an organic, or integral, American Architecture.

Of course, it is just as easy to cheat by simplicity as it is to cheat with "classical" structure. So, unluckily, here again is the "modernistic" architectural picture-maker's deadly facility for imitation at ease and again too happy with fresh opportunity to "fake effects." Probably another Renaissance is here imminent.

Architecture is now integral architecture only when Plasticity is a genuine expression of actual construction just as the articulate line and surface of the hand is articulate of the structure of the hand. Arriving at steel, I first used Continuity as actual stabilizing principle in concrete slabs, and in the concrete ferro-block system I devised in Los Angeles.

In the form of the cantilever or as horizontal continuity this new economy by means of tenuity is what saved the Imperial Hotel from destruction, but it did not appear in the grammar of the building for various reasons, chiefly because the building was to look somewhat as though it belonged to Tokyo.

Later, in the new design for St. Mark's Tower, New York City, this new working principle economized material, labor, and liberated or liberalized space in a more developed sense. It gave to the structure the significant outlines of remarkable stability and instead of false masonry-mass significant outlines came out. The abstract pattern of the structure as a complete structural-integrity of Form and Idea may be seen fused as in any tree but with nothing imitating a tree.

Continuity invariably realized remarkable economy of labor and building materials as well as space. Unfortunately there is yet little or no data to use as tabulation. Tests will have to be made continually for many years to make the record available to slide-rule engineers.

In the ancient order there was little thought of economy of materials. The more massive the whole structure looked, the better it looked to the ancients. But seen in the light of these new economic interior forces conserved by the tensile strength of a sheet of plastic or any interweaving of strands of steel in this machine age, the old order was as sick with weight as the Buonarotti dome. Weak . . . because there could be no co-interrelation between the two elements of support and supported to reinforce each other as a whole under stress or elemental disturbance.

So this tremendous new resource of *tenuity*—a quality of steel —this quality of *pull* in a building (you may see it ushering in a new era in John Roebling's Brooklyn Bridge) was definitely lacking in all ancient architecture because steel had not been born into building.

The tenuous strand or slab as a common means of strength had yet to come. Here today this element of continuity may cut structural substance nearly in two. It may cut the one half in two again by elimination of needless features, such elimination being entirely due to the simplification I have been calling "plasticity."

It is by utilizing mass production in the factory in this connection that some idea of the remarkable new economics possible to modern architecture may be seen approaching those realized in any well-built machine. If standardization can be humanized and made flexible in design and the economics brought to the home owner, the greatest service will be rendered to our modern way of life. It may be really born—this democracy, I mean.

Involved as a matter of design in this mass production, however, are the involute, all but involuntary reactions to which I have just referred: the ipso facto building code and the fact that the building engineer as now trained knows so little about them. However, the engineer is learning to calculate by model-making in some instances—notably Professor Beggs at Princeton.

The codes so far as I can see will have to die on the vine with the men who made them.

MATERIALS FOR THEIR OWN SAKE

As the first integrity and the two first new resources appeared out of the interior nature of the kind of building, called Architecture—so now, naturally, interior to the true nature of any good building, comes the fourth new resource. This is found by recognizing the nature of the materials used in construction.

Just as many fascinating different properties as there are different materials that may be used to build a building will continually and naturally qualify, modify and utterly change all architectural form whatsoever.

A stone building will no more *be* nor will it *look* like a steel building. A pottery, or terra cotta building, will not be nor should it look like a stone building. A wood building will look like none other, for it will glorify the stick. A steel and glass building could not possibly look like anything but itself. It will glorify steel and glass. And so on all the way down the long list of available riches in materials: Stone, Wood, Concrete, Metals, Glass, Textiles, Pulp and Plastics; riches so great to our hand today that no comparison with Ancient Architecture is at all sensible or anything but obstruction to our Modern Architecture.

In this particular, as you may see, architecture is going back to learn from the natural source of all natural things.

In order to get Organic Architecture born, intelligent architects will be forced to turn their backs on antique rubbish heaps with which Classic eclecticism has encumbered our new ground. So far as architecture has gone in my own thought it is first of all a character and quality of *mind* that may enter also into human conduct with social implications that might, at first, confound or astound you. But the only basis for any fear of them lies in the fact that they are all sanely and thoroughly *constructive*.

Instinctively all forms of pretense fear and hate reality. THE HYPOCRITE MUST ALWAYS HATE THE RADICAL.

This potent fourth new resource—the Nature of Materials— gets at the common center of every material in relation to the work it is required to do. This means that the architect must again begin at the very beginning. Proceeding according to Nature now he must sensibly go through with whatever material may be in hand for his purpose according to the methods and sensibilities of a man in this age. And when I say Nature, I mean inherent *structure* seen always by the architect as a matter of complete design. It is in itself, always, *nature-pattern.* It is this profound internal sense of materials that enters in as Architecture now. It is this, the fifth new resource, that must captivate and hold the mind of the modern architect to creative work. The fifth will give new life to his imagination if it has not been already killed at school.

And, inevitable implication! New machine-age resources require that all buildings do *not* resemble each other. The new ideal does *not* require that all buildings be of steel, concrete or glass. Often that might be idiotic waste.

Nor do the resources even *imply* that mass is no longer a beautiful attribute of masonry materials when they are genuinely used. We are entitled to a vast variety of form in our complex age so long as the form be genuine—serves Architecture and Architecture serves life.

But in this land of ours, richest on earth of all in old and new materials, architects must exercise well-trained imagination to see in each material, either natural or compounded plastics, their own *inherent style.* All materials may be beautiful, their beauty much or entirely depending upon how well they are used by the Architect.

In our modern building we have the Stick. Stone. Steel. Pottery. Concrete. Glass. Yes, Pulp, too, as well as plastics. And since this dawning sense of the "within" is the new reality, these will all give the main *motif* for any real building made from them. The materials of which the building is built will go far to determine its appropriate mass, its outline and, especially, proportion. *Character* is criterion in the form of any and every building or industrial product we can call Architecture in the light of this new ideal of the new order.

THE NEW INTEGRITY

Strange! At this late date, it is modern architecture that wants life to learn to see life as life, because architecture must learn to see brick as brick, learn to see steel as steel, see glass as glass. So modern thought urges all of life to demand that a bank look like a bank (bad thought though a bank might become) and not depend upon false columns for credit. The new architecture urges all of life to demand that an office building look like an office building, even if it should resemble the cross section of a bee-hive. Life itself should sensibly insist in self-defense that a hotel look and conduct itself like a hotel and not like some office building. Life should declare, too, that the railroad station look like a railroad station and not try so hard to look like an ancient temple or some monarchic palazzo. And while we are on this subject, why not a place for opera that would look something like a place for opera —if we must have opera, and not look so much like a gilded, crimsoned bagnio. Life declares that a filling station should stick to its work as a filling station: look the part becomingly. Why try to look like some Colonial diminutive or remain just a pump on the street. Although "just a pump" on the street is better than the Colonial imitation. The good Life itself demands that the school be as generously spaced and a thought-built good-time place for happy children: a building no more than one story high—with some light overhead, the school building should regard the children as a garden in sun. Life itself demands of Modern Architecture that the house of a man who knows what home is should have his own home his own way if we have any man left in that connection after F.H.A. is done trying to put them, all of them it can, into the case of a man who builds a home only to sell it. Our Government forces the home-maker into the real-estate business if he wants a home at all.

Well, after all, this line of thought was all new-type common sense in architecture in Chicago only thirty years ago. It began to grow up in my own work as it is continuing to grow up more and more widely in the work of all the world. But, insulting as it may seem to say so, nor is it merely arrogant to say that the actual thinking in that connection is still a novelty, only a little less strange today than it was then, although the appearances do rapidly increase.

INTEGRAL ORNAMENT AT LAST!

At last, is this fifth resource, so old yet now demanding fresh significance. We have arrived at integral ornament—the nature-pattern of actual construction. Here, confessed as the spiritual demand for true significancé, comes this subjective element in modern architecture. An element so hard to understand that modern architects themselves seem to understand it least well of all and most of them have turned against it with such fury as is born only of impotence.

And it *is* true that this vast, intensely human significance is really no matter at all for any but the most imaginative mind not without some development in artistry and the *gift* of a sense of proportion. Certainly we must go higher in the realm of imagination when we presume to enter here, because we go into Poetry.

Now, very many write good prose who cannot write poetry at all. And although staccato specification is the present fashion, just as "functionalist" happens to be the present style in writing—

poetic prose will never be undesirable. But who condones prosaic poetry? None. Not even those fatuously condemned to write it.

So, I say this fourth new resource and the fifth demand for new significance and integrity is ornament *integral to building as itself poetry*. Rash use of a dangerous word. The word "Poetry" *is* a dangerous word.

Heretofore, I have used the word "pattern" instead of the word ornament to avoid confusion or to escape the passing prejudice. But here now ornament is in its place. Ornament meaning not only *surface qualified by human imagination* but imagination giving *natural pattern* to structure. Perhaps this phrase says it all without further explanation. This resource—integral ornament—is new in the architecture of the world, at least insofar not only as imagination qualifying a surface—a valuable resource—but as a greater means than that: *imagination giving natural pattern to structure itself*. Here we have new significance, indeed! Long ago this significance was lost to the scholarly architect. A man of taste. He, too, soon, became content with symbols.

Evidently then, this expression of structure as a pattern true to the nature of the materials out of which it was made, may be taken much further along than physical need alone would dictate? "If you have a loaf of bread break the loaf in two and give the half of it for some flowers of the Narcissus, for the bread feeds the body indeed but the flowers feed the soul."

Into these higher realms of imagination associated in the popular mind as sculpture and painting, buildings may be as fully taken by modern means today as they ever were by craftsmen of the antique order.

It is by this last and poetic resource that we may give greater structural entity and greater human significance to the whole building than could ever be done otherwise. This statement is heresy at this left-wing moment, so—we ask, "taken how and when taken?" I confess you may well ask by whom? The answer is, taken by the true *poet.* And where is this Poet today? Time will answer.

Yet again in this connection let us remember Ong's Chinese observation, "Poetry is the sound of the heart." So, in the same uncommon sense integral ornament is the developed sense of the building as a whole, or the manifest *abstract pattern of structure itself.* Interpreted. Integral ornament is simply *structure-pattern made visibly articulate* and seen in the building as it is seen articulate in the structure of the trees or a lily of the fields. It is the expression of inner rhythm of Form. Are we talking about Style? Pretty nearly. At any rate, we are talking about the qualities that make *essential architecture* as distinguished from any mere act of building whatsoever.

What I am here calling integral ornament is founded upon the same organic simplicities as Beethoven's Fifth Symphony, that amazing revolution in tumult and splendor of sound built on four tones based upon a rhythm a child could play on the piano with one finger. Supreme imagination reared the four repeated tones, simple rhythms, into a great symphonic poem that is probably the noblest thought-built edifice in our world. And Architecture is like Music in this capacity for the symphony.

But concerning higher development of building to more completely express its life principle as significant and beautiful, let us say at once by way of warning: it is better to die by the wayside of left-wing Ornaphobia than it is to build any more merely ornamented buildings, as such; or to see right-wing architects die any more ignoble deaths of *Ornamentia.* All period and pseudo-classic buildings whatever, and (although their authors do not seem to know it) most protestant buildings, they call themselves internationalist, are really ornamental in definitely objectionable sense. A plain flat surface cut to shape for its own sake, however large or plain the shape, is, the moment it is sophisticatedly so cut, no less ornamental than egg-and-dart. All such buildings are objectionably "ornamental," because like any buildings of the old classical order both wholly ignore the *nature* of the *first* integrity. Both also ignore the four resources and both neglect the nature of machines at work on materials. Incidentally and as a matter of course both misjudge the nature of time, place and the modern life of man.

Here in this new leftish emulation as we now have it, is only the "istic," ignoring principle merely to get the "look" of the machine or something that looks "new." The province of the "ite."

In most so-called "internationalist" or "modernistic" building therefore we have no true approach to organic architecture: we have again merely a new, superficial esthetic trading upon that architecture because such education as most of our architects possess qualifies them for only some kind of eclecticism past, passing, or to pass.

Nevertheless I say, if we can't have buildings with integrity we would better have more imitation machines for buildings until we can have truly sentient architecture. "The machine for living in" is sterile, but therefore it is safer, I believe, than the festering mass of ancient styles.

GREAT POWER

A far greater power than slavery, even the intellectual slavery as in the school of the Greeks, is back of these five demands for machine-age significance and integrity. Stupendous and stupefying power. That power is the leverage of the machine itself. As now set up in all its powers the machine will confirm these new implicities and complicities in architecture at every point, but will destroy them soon if not checked by a new simplicity.

The proper use of these new resources demands that we use them all together with integrity for mankind if we are to realize the finer significances of life. The finer significance, prophesied if not realized by organic architecture. It *is* reasonable to believe that life in our country will be lived in full enjoyment of this new freedom of the extended horizontal line because the horizontal line now becomes the great architectural highway. The flat plane now becomes the regional field. And integral-pattern becomes "the sound of the Usonian* heart."

I see this extended horizontal line as the true earth-line of human life, indicative of freedom. Always.

The broad expanded plane is the horizontal plane infinitely extended. In that lies such freedom for man on this earth as he may call his.

This new sense of Architecture as integral-pattern of that type and kind may awaken these United States to fresh beauty, and the Usonian horizon of the individual will be immeasurably extended by enlightened use of this great lever, the machine. But only if it gets into creative hands loyal to humanity.

*Usonia was Samuel Butler's name for the United States.

First design for Dean Malcolm Willey House in Minneapolis. Living room and kitchen workspace on roof-deck, bedroom on the garden level. Cost in 1934: $16,000.

The plan and photographs shown on the following pages are of "The Garden Wall": house built in 1934 for Dean Malcolm Willey—Nancy Willey, Superintendent. Cost: $10,000. A well-protected brick house built upon a brick paved 3 in. concrete mat laid down over well drained bed of cinders and sand—the concrete mat jointed at partitions. To develop the nature of the materials a sand mold brick course alternates with a course of paving brick, the exterior cypress is left to weather and the interior cypress is only waxed.

The house wraps around the northwest corner of a lot sloping to the south—a fine vista in that direction. The plan protects the Willeys from the neighbors, sequesters a small garden and realizes the view to the utmost under good substantial shelter. Notwithstanding the protests of the builder and unusually many kind friends, the fireplace draws perfectly and the mat is perfectly comfortable in 30° below zero weather. Nor does the frost show upon the inside of the outside walls. The house emphasizes the modern sense of space by vista inside and outside, without getting at all "modernistic." There is a well balanced interpenetration (that is to say, sense of proportion) of the sense of shelter with this sense of space, the sense of materials and the purpose of the whole structure in this dwelling. It is well constructed for a life of several centuries if the shingle roof is renewed in twenty-five years or tile is substituted. Perhaps this northern house comes as near to being permanent human shelter as any family of this transitory period is entitled to expect.

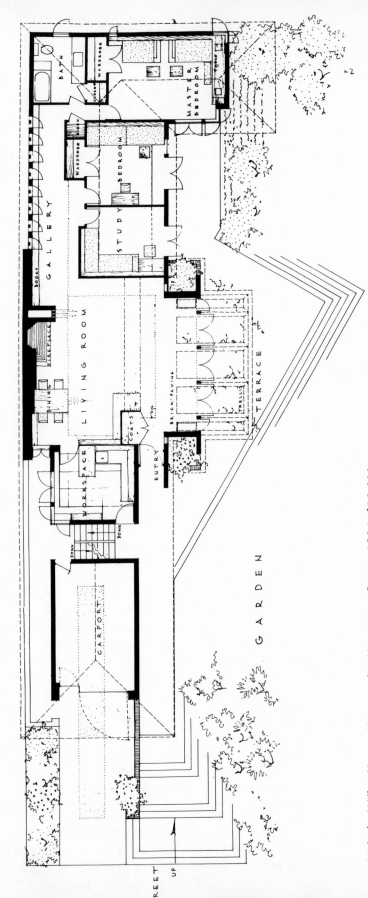

Malcolm Willey House, Minneapolis, Minnesota. Cost in 1934: $10,000.

WILLEY HOUSE FROM SOUTH.
ALTERNATING LAYERS OF DARK RED SAND MOLD AND PAVING BRICK IN PAVEMENTS, WALLS, FIREPLACE.

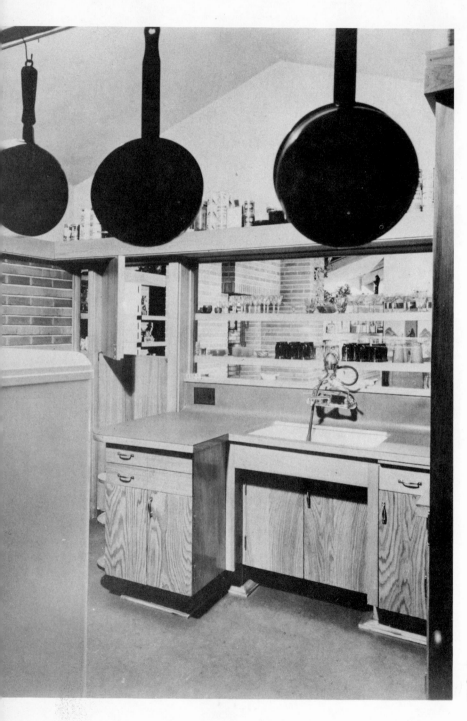

Glass walled work-unit looks out upon
dining area and living room fireplace
beyond.

Book lined corridor. Floor mat brick-
paved. Waxed cypress members sash
and doors.

DINING TABLE ARRANGEMENT NEAR FIREPLACE BESIDE GLASS SCREEN TO WORKSPACE.

RED BRICK FIREPLACE IN LIVING ROOM. SAME ALTERNATING BRICK COURSES IN FLOORS AND WALLS.

VIEW IN EARLY NOVEMBER. LOOKING TO NORTH. GLAZED DOORS TO LIVING ROOM AND WOOD TRELLIS OVER.

THE USONIAN HOUSE I

The house of moderate cost is not only America's major architectural problem but the problem most difficult for her major architects. As for me, I would rather solve it with satisfaction to myself and Usonia, than build anything I can think of at the moment except the modern theater now needed by the legitimate drama unless the stage is to be done to death by "the movies." In our country the chief obstacle to any real solution of the moderate-cost house problem is the fact that our people do not really know how to live. They imagine their idiosyncrasies to be their "tastes," their prejudices to be their predilections, and their ignorance to be virtue—where any beauty of living is concerned.

To be more specific, a small house on the side street might have charm if it didn't ape the big house on the Avenue, just as the Usonian village itself might have a great charm if it didn't ape the big town. Likewise, Marybud on the old farm, a jewel hanging from the tip of her pretty nose on a cold, cold day, might be charming in clothes befitting her state and her work, but is only silly in the Sears-Roebuck finery that imitates the clothes of her city sisters who imitate Hollywood stars: lipstick, rouge, high heels, silk stockings, bell skirt, cockeyed hat, and all. Exactly that kind of "monkey-fied" business is the obstacle to architectural achievement in our U.S.A. This provincial "culture-lag" in favor of the lag which does not allow the person, thing, or thought to be simple and naturally itself. It is the real obstacle to a genuine Usonian culture.

I am certain that any approach to the new house needed by indigenous culture—why worry about the house wanted by provincial "tasteful" ignorance!—is fundamentally different. That house must be a pattern for more simplified and, at the same time, more gracious living: necessarily new, but suitable to living conditions as they might so well be in this country we live in today.

This need of a house of moderate cost must sometime face not only expedients but Reality. Why not face it now? The expedient houses built by the million, which journals propagate, and government builds, do no such thing.

To me such houses are stupid makeshifts, putting on some style or other, really having no integrity. Style *is* important. *A* style is not. There is all the difference when we work *with* style and not for *a* style.

I have insisted on that point for forty-five years.

Notwithstanding all efforts to improve the product, the American "small house" problem is still a pressing, needy, hungry, confused issue. But where is a better thing to come from while Authority has pitched into perpetuating the old supidities? I do not believe the needed house can come from current education, or from big business. It isn't coming by way of smart advertising experts either. Or professional streamliners. It is only super-common-sense that can take us along the road to the better thing in building.

What would be really sensible in this matter of the modest dwelling for our time and place? Let's see how far the first Herbert Jacobs house at Madison, Wisconsin, is a sensible house. This house for a young journalist, his wife, and small daughter, was built in 1937. Cost: Fifty-five hundred dollars, including architect's fee of four hundred and fifty. Contract let to P. B. Grove.

To give the small Jacobs family the benefit of the advantages of the era in which they live, many simplifications must take place. Mr. and Mrs. Jacobs must themselves see life in somewhat simplified terms. What are essentials in their case, a typical case? It is not only necessary to get rid of all unnecessary complications in construction, necessary to use work in the mill to good advantage, necessary to eliminate, so far as possible, field labor which is always expensive: it is necessary to consolidate and simplify the three appurtenance systems—heating, lighting, and sanitation. At least this must be our economy if we are to achieve the sense of spaciousness and vista we desire in order to liberate the people living in the house. And it would be ideal to complete the building in one operation as it goes along. Inside and outside should be complete in one operation. The house finished inside as it is completed outside. There should be no complicated roofs.

Every time a hip or a valley or a dormer window is allowed to ruffle a roof the life of the building is threatened.

The way the windows are used is naturally a most useful resource to achieve the new characteristic sense of space. All this fenestration can be made ready at the factory and set up as the walls. But there is no longer sense in speaking of doors and windows. These walls are largely a system of fenestration having its own part in the building scheme—the system being as much a part of the design as eyes are part of the face.

Now what can be eliminated? These:

1. Visible roofs are expensive and unnecessary.

2. A garage is no longer necessary as cars are made. A carport will do, with liberal over-head shelter and walls on two sides. Detroit still has the livery-stable mind. It believes that the car is a horse and must be stabled.

3. The old-fashioned basement, except for a fuel and heater

Preliminary sketches of Jacobs house. First house with gravity heat. Steam pipes in the floor slab. 1937.

space, was always a plague spot. A steam-warmed concrete mat four inches thick laid directly on the ground over gravel filling, the walls set upon that, is better.

4. Interior "trim" is no longer necessary.

5. We need no radiators, no light fixtures. We will heat the house the "hypocaust" way—in or between the floors. We can make the wiring system itself be the light fixture, throwing light upon and down the ceiling. Light will thus be indirect, except for a few outlets for floor lamps.

6. Furniture, pictures and bric-a-brac are unnecessary because the walls can be made to include them or *be* them.

7. No painting at all. Wood best preserves itself. A coating of clear resinous oil would be enough. Only the floor mat of concrete squares needs waxing.

8. No plastering in the building.

9. No gutters, no downspouts.

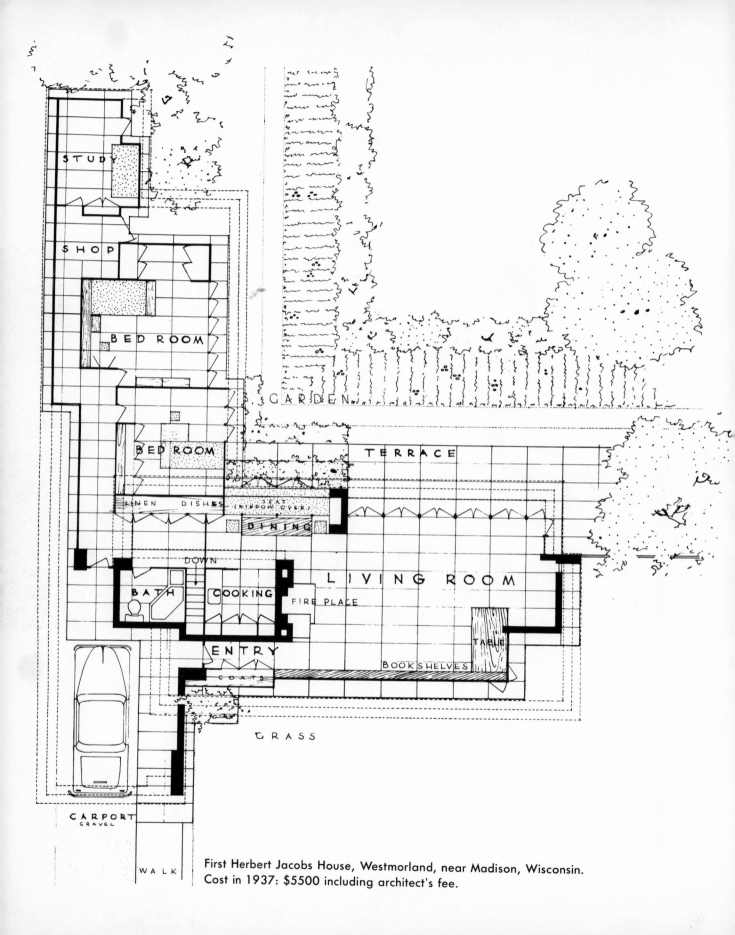

STUDY

SHOP

BED ROOM

GARDEN

BED ROOM

TERRACE

LINEN   DISHES   SEAT (WINDOW OVER)

DINING

DOWN

LIVING ROOM

BATH   COOKING   FIRE PLACE

ENTRY

TABLE

BOOKSHELVES

COATS

GRASS

CARPORT
GRAVEL

WALK

First Herbert Jacobs House, Westmorland, near Madison, Wisconsin.
Cost in 1937: $5500 including architect's fee.

To assist in general planning, what must or may we use in our new construction? In this case five materials: wood, brick, cement, paper, glass. To simplify fabrication we must use our horizontal-unit system in construction. We must also use a vertical-unit system which will be the widths of the boards and batten-bands themselves, interlocking with the brick courses. Although it is getting to be a luxury material, the walls will be wood board-walls the same

Jacobs house. This Usonian house turns its back on the street, to secure privacy for the indwellers.

inside as outside—three thicknesses of boards with paper placed between them, the boards fastened together with screws. These slab-walls of boards—a kind of plywood construction on a large scale can be high in insulating value, vermin-proof, and practically fireproof. These walls like the fenestration may be prefabricated on the floor, with any degree of insulation we can afford, and raised into place, or they may be made at the mill and shipped to

85

the site in sections. The roof can be built first on props and these walls shoved into place under them.

The appurtenance systems, to avoid cutting and complications, must be an organic part of construction but independent of the

walls. Yes, we must have polished plate glass. It is one of the things we have at hand to gratify the designer of the truly modern house and bless its occupants.

The roof framing in this instance is laminated of three 2 x 4's in depth easily making the three offsets seen outside in the eaves of the roof, and enabling the roof span of 2 x 12″ to be sufficiently pitched without the expense of "building up" the pitches. The middle offset may be left open at the eaves and fitted with flaps

used to ventilate the roof spaces in summer. These 2 x 4's sheathed and insulated, then covered with a good asphalt roof, are the top of the house, shelter gratifying to the sense of shelter because of the generous eaves.

All this is in hand—no, it is in mind, as we plan the disposition of the rooms.

What must we consider essential now? We have a corner lot— say, an acre or two— with a south and west exposure? We will have a good garden. The house is planned to wrap around two sides of this garden.

1. We must have as big a living room with as much vista and garden coming in as we can afford, with a fireplace in it,

and open bookshelves, a dining table in the alcove, benches, and living-room tables built in; a quiet rug on the floor.

2. Convenient cooking and dining space adjacent to if not a part of the living room. This space may be set away from the outside walls within the living area to make work easy. This is the new thought concerning a kitchen—to take it away

from outside walls and let it turn up into overhead space within the chimney; thus connection to dining space is made immediate without unpleasant features and no outside wall space lost to the principal rooms. A natural current of air is thus set up toward the kitchen as toward a chimney, no cooking odors escaping back into the house. There are steps leading down from this space to a small cellar below for heater, fuel, and laundry, although no basement at all is necessary if the plan should be so made. The bathroom is usually next so that plumbing features of heating kitchen and bath may be economically combined.

3. In this case (two bedrooms and a workshop which may become a future bedroom) the single bathroom for the sake of privacy is not immediately connected to any single bedroom. Bathrooms opening directly into a bedroom occupied by more than one person or two bedrooms opening into a single bathroom have been badly overdone. We will have as much garden and space in all these space appropriations as our money allows after we have simplified construction by way of the technique we have tried out.

A modest house, this Usonian house, a dwelling place that has no feeling at all for the "grand" except as the house extends itself in the flat parallel to the ground. It will be a companion to the horizon. With floor-heating that kind of extension on the ground can hardly go too far for comfort or beauty of proportion, provided it does not cost too much in upkeep. As a matter of course a home like this is an architect's creation. It is not a builder's nor an amateur's effort. There is considerable risk in exposing the scheme to imitation or emulation.

This is true because a house of this type could not be well built and achieve its design except as an architect oversees the building.

And the building would fail of proper effect unless the furnishing and planting were all done by advice of the architect.

Thus briefly these few descriptive paragraphs together with the plan may help to indicate how stuffy and stifling the little colonial hot-boxes, hallowed by government or not, really are where Usonian family life is concerned. You might easily put two of them, each costing more, into the living space of this one and not go much outside the walls. Here is a moderate-cost brick-and-wood house that by our new technology has been greatly extended both in scale and comfort: a single house suited to prefabrication because the factory can go to the house.

Imagine how the costs would come down were the technique a familiar matter or if many houses were to be executed at one time

THE JACOBS HOUSE FROM THE INTERIOR GARDEN.

—probably down to forty-five hundred dollars, according to number built and location.

There is a freedom of movement, and a privacy too, afforded by the general arrangement here that is unknown to the current "boxment." Let us say nothing about beauty. Beauty is an ambiguous term concerning an affair of taste in the provinces of which our big cities are the largest.

But I think a cultured American, we say Usonian, housewife will look well in it. The now inevitable car will seem a part of it.

Where does the garden leave off and the house begin? Where the garden begins and the house leaves off.

Withal, this Usonian dwelling seems a thing loving the ground with the new sense of space, light, and freedom—to which our U.S.A. is entitled.

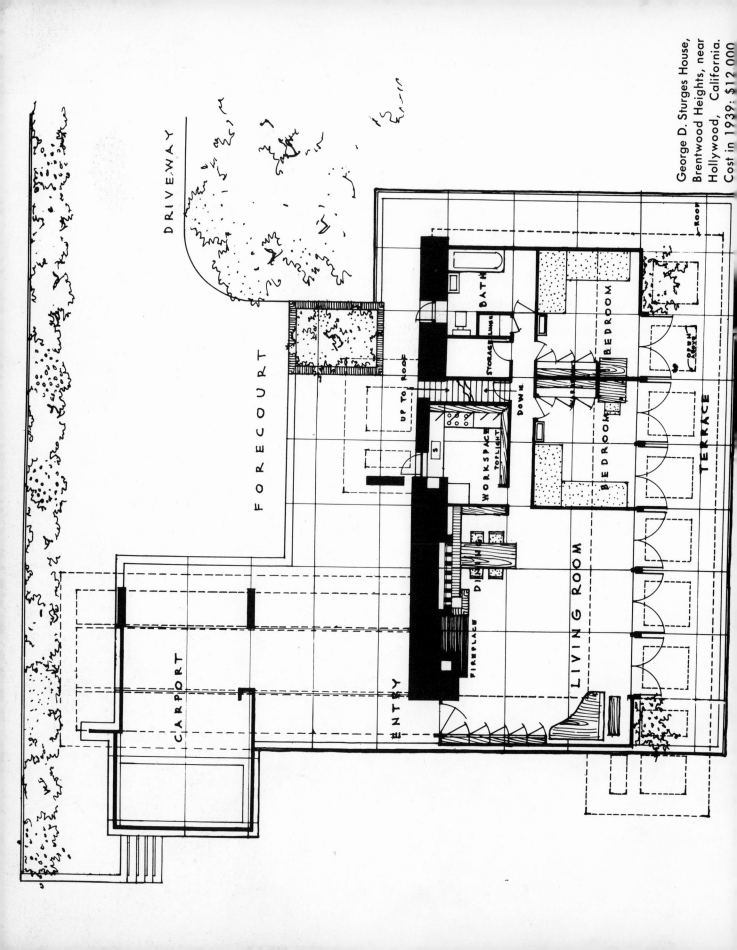

George D. Sturges House,
Brentwood Heights, near
Hollywood, California.
Cost in 1939: $12.000

STURGES HOUSE, FACING SOUTHWEST TOWARD OCEAN.

STURGES HOUSE. DINING TABLE ARRANGEMENT BETWEEN WORKSPACE AND LIVING ROOM FIREPLACE.

STURGES HOUSE, OF REDWOOD, CANTILEVERED OVER STEEP BANK FROM BRICK WALL MASSES.

THE USONIAN HOUSE II

We have built over a hundred of them now in nearly all our states. Building costs in general in the U.S.A. were rising and are rising still.* We find that twenty thousand dollars is about the sum needed to do what the Jacobs bought for fifty-five hundred. The Usonian house would have cost from twelve, and in some certain extensive programs, on up to seventy-five thousand dollars. We have built several extended in every way that cost more than one hundred thousand.

The houses cost a good deal more to build now than when we started to build them in 1938. But this holds true—any comparison with the "regular" houses around them shows that they are more for the money physically for the sums they cost than the "regulars" around about them. Their freedom, distinction, and individuality are not a feature of that cost except as it does, by elimination, put the expenditure where it liberates the occupant in a new spaciousness. A new freedom.

It is true however that no man can have the liberation one of these houses affords with liberal outside views on three sides becoming a part of the interior, without incurring extra fuel—say

*Brought up to date by Frank Lloyd Wright, 1954

97

twenty per cent more. Double windows cut this down—but also cost money.

GRAVITY HEAT

Concerning floor heating. Heated air naturally rises. We call it gravity heat because the pipes filled with steam or hot water are all in a rock ballast bed beneath the concrete floor—we call the ballast with concrete top, the floor mat. If the floor is above the ground it is made of two-inch-square wood strips spaced 3′ 8″ apart. The heating pipes are in that case set between the floor joists.

It came to me in this way: In Japan to commence building the new Imperial Hotel, winter of 1914, we were invited to dine with Baron Okura, one of my patrons. It is desperately cold in Tokyo in winter—a damp clammy cold that almost never amounts to freezing or frost, but it is harder to keep warm there than anywhere else I have been, unless in Italy. The universal heater is the *hibachi*—a round vessel sitting on the floor filled with white ashes, several sticks of charcoal thrust down into the ashes all but a few inches. This projecting charcoal is lighted and glows—incandescent. Everyone sits around the *hibachi,* every now and then stretching out the hand over it for a moment—closing the hand as though grasping at something. The result is very unsatisfactory. To us. I marveled at Japanese fortitude until I caught sight of the typical underwear —heavy woolens, long sleeves, long legs, which they wear beneath the series of padded flowing kimono. But as they are acclimated and toughened to this native condition they suffer far less than we do.

Well, although we knew we should shiver, we accepted the invitation to dine at Baron Okura's Tokyo house—he had a number of houses scattered around the Empire. As expected, the dining room was so cold that I couldn't eat—pretending to eat only and for some nineteen courses. After dinner the Baron led the way below to the "Korean room," as it was called. This room was about eleven by fifteen, ceiling seven feet, I should say. A red-felt drugget covered the floor mats. The walls were severely plain, a soft pale yellow in color. We knelt there for conversation and Turkish coffee.

The climate seemed to have changed. No, it wasn't the coffee; it was Spring. We were soon warm and happy again—kneeling there on the floor, an indescribable warmth. No heating was visible nor was it felt directly as such. It was really a matter *not of heating at all* but an affair of *climate*.

The Harvard graduate who interpreted for the Baron explained: the Korean room meant a room heated under the floor. The heat of a fire outside at one corner of the floor drawn back and forth underneath the floor in and between tile ducts, the floor forming the top of the flues (or ducts) made by the partitions, the smoke and heat going up and out of a tall chimney at the corner opposite the corner where the fire was burning.

The indescribable comfort of being warmed from below was a discovery.

I immediately arranged for electric heating elements beneath the bathrooms in the Imperial Hotel—dropping the ceiling of the bathrooms to create a space beneath each in which to generate the heat. The tile floor and built-in tile baths were thus always warm. It was pleasant to go in one's bare feet into the bath. This experiment was a success. All ugly electric heat fixtures (dangerous too in a bathroom) were eliminated. I've always hated fixtures —radiators especially. Here was the complete opportunity to digest all that paraphernalia in the building—creating not a heated interior but creating climate—healthful, dustless, serene. And also, the presence of heat thus integral and beneath makes lower temperatures desirable. Sixty-five degrees seems for normal human beings sufficient. But neighbors coming in from super-heated houses would feel the cold at first. It is true that a natural climate is generated instead of an artificial forced condition—the natural condition much more healthful, as a matter of course.

I determined to try it out at home at the first opportunity. That opportunity seemed to be the Nakoma Country Club but that Indianesque affair stayed in the form of a beautiful plan.

Then came the Johnson Administration Building. Just the thing for that and we proceeded with the installation, but all the professional heating contractors except one (Westerlin and Campbell) scoffed, refusing to have anything to do with the idea. But as chance had it, the little Jacobs House turned up meantime and was completed before that greater venture got into operation.

So the Jacobs House was the first installation to go into effect. There was great excitement and curiosity on the part of the "profession." Crane Company officials came in, dove beneath the rugs, put their hands on the concrete in places remote from the heater, got up and looked at one another as though they had seen a ghost. My God! It works. Where were radiators now?

As usual.

Articles on "radiant heat" began to appear in testimonial journals. But it was in no sense "radiant heat" or panel heating or any of the things they called it that I was now interested in. It was simply *gravity heat*—heat coming up from beneath as naturally as heat rises.

Many of the Usonian buildings now have floor heating. We have had to learn to proportion the heat correctly for varying climates and conditions. We have accumulated some data that is useful.

There is no other "ideal" heat. Not even the heat of the sun.

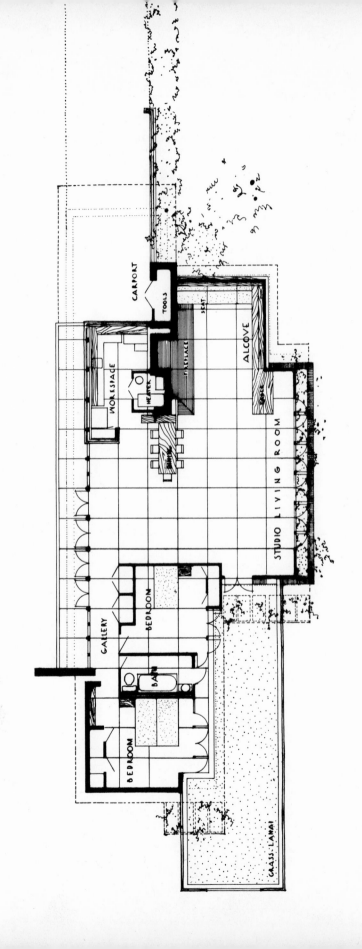

Goetsch-Winkler House, Okemos, Michigan. Cost in 1939: $9500.

GOETSCH-WINKLER HOUSE, VIEW FROM NORTHEAST.

"Gratifying to the sense of shelter because of the generous eaves" . . . over glass doors to living room of Goetsch-Winkler House.

GOETSCH-WINKLER HOUSE, VIEW FROM SOUTHEAST. OPEN WINDOWS OF STUDIO LIVING ROOM.

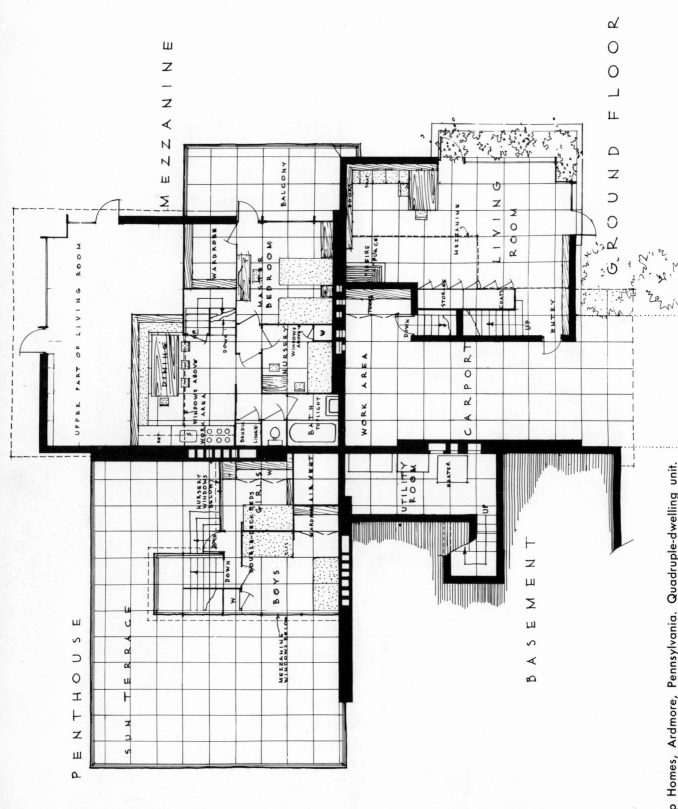

Suntop Homes, Ardmore, Pennsylvania. Quadruple-dwelling unit.
Cost in 1939: about $16,000 for all four dwellings.

SUNTOP HOMES. ARDMORE. PENNSYLVANIA.

SUNTOP HOMES, ARDMORE, PENNSYLVANIA.

The plan on the following page was for a housing project on a 100 acre tract near Pittsfield, Massachusetts, for the United States Government. In this scheme of cloverleaf ground subdivision, standardization is no barrier to the quality of infinite variety to be observed in nature. In these quadruple units no entrance to any dwelling in the group of 100 houses is beside any other entrance to another dwelling. So far as any individual can know, the entire group is his home. He is entirely unaware of the activities of his neighbors. There is no looking from front windows to backyards: all the private functions of family life are here independent of those of any other family. Playgrounds for the children, called sundecks, are small roof gardens placed where the mother of the family has direct supervision over hers. Family processes are conveniently centralized on the mezzanine next to the master bedroom and bath where the mistress of the house can turn a pancake with one hand while putting the baby into a bath with the other, father meantime sitting at his dinner, lord of it all, daughter meantime having the privacy of the front room below for the entertainment of her friends.

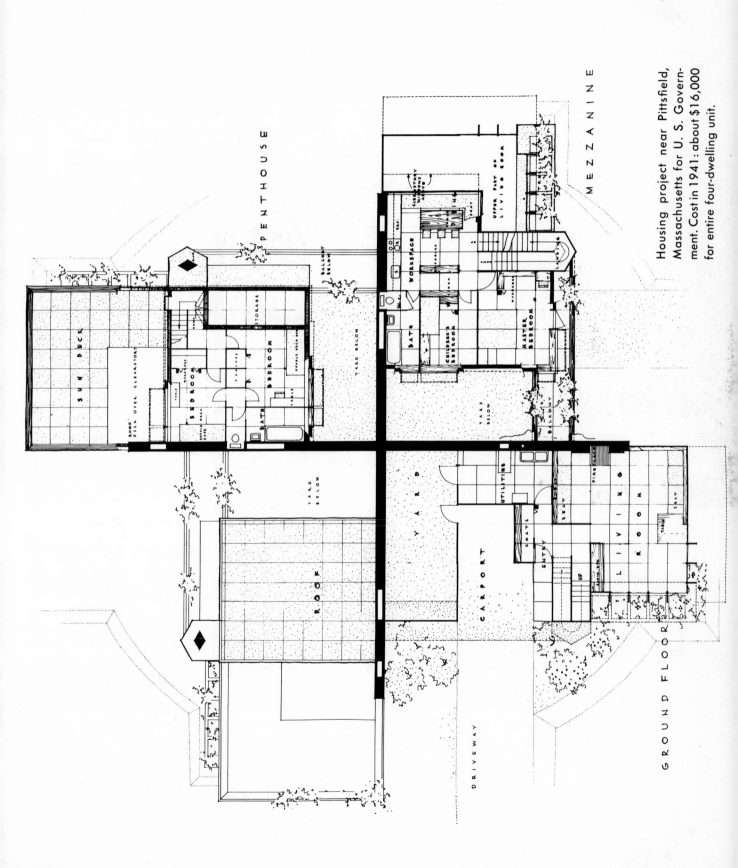

Housing project near Pittsfield, Massachusetts for U. S. Government. Cost in 1941: about $16,000 for entire four-dwelling unit.

PENTHOUSE

MEZZANINE

SUN DECK

Roof Deck over Clearstory

BEDROOM

BATH

STORAGE

BALCONY BELOW

YARD BELOW

CLEARSTORY BELOW

WORKSPACE

BATH

CHILDREN'S BEDROOM

UPPER PART OF LIVING ROOM

MASTER BEDROOM

LANDING

BALCONY

YARD BELOW

ROOF

YARD BELOW

Y A R D

CARPORT

DRIVEWAY

UTILITIES

SEAT

FIREPLACE

ENTRY

COATS

SEAT

UP

L I V I N G   R O O M

SEAT

G R O U N D   F L O O R

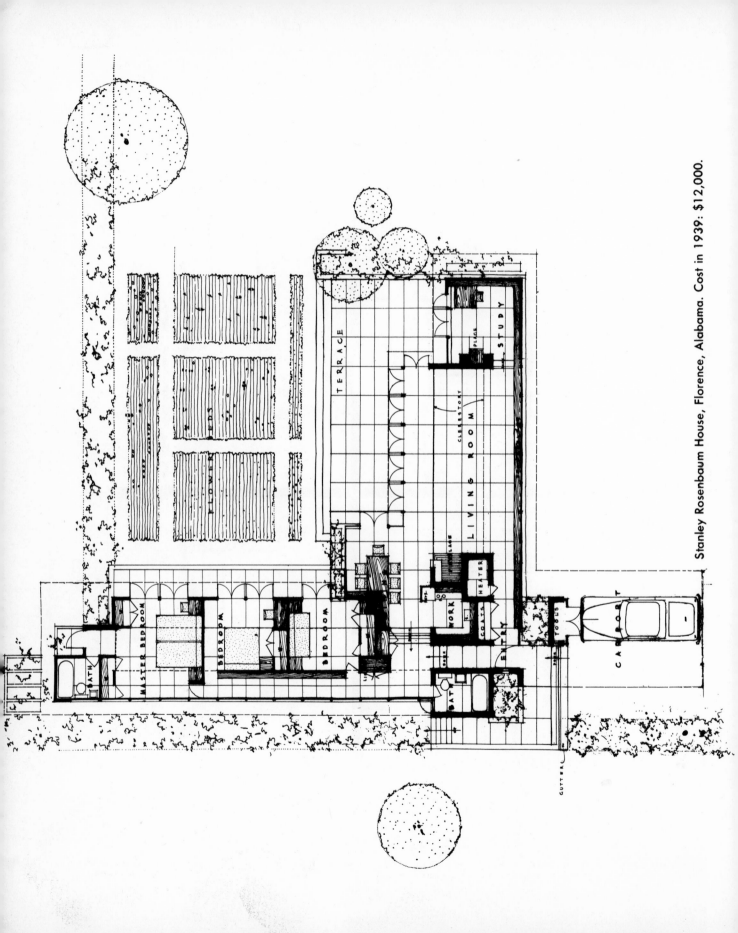

Stanley Rosenbaum House, Florence, Alabama. Cost in 1939: $12,000.

ROSENBAUM HOUSE. GLASS DOORS TO LIVING ROOM AT LEFT TO BEDROOMS AT RIGHT.

ROSENBAUM HOUSE, REAR VIEW.

DINING TABLE ARRANGEMENT IN ROSENBAUM HOUSE.

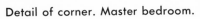
Detail of corner. Master bedroom.

ROSENBAUM HOUSE, LIVING ROOM, CLERESTORY ABOVE.

CONCERNING THE USONIAN HOUSE

This statement was written by Mr. Wright for the opening of the Usonian House in the exhibition, Sixty Years of Living Architecture: The Work of Frank Lloyd Wright, at The Solomon R. Guggenheim Museum, New York, November 1953.

To say the house planted by myself on the good earth of the Chicago prairie as early as 1900, or earlier, was the first truly democratic expression of our democracy in Architecture would start a controversy with professional addicts who believe Architecture has no political (therefore no social) significance. So, let's say that the spirit of democracy—freedom of the individual as an individual—took hold of the house as it then was, took off the attic and the porch, pulled out the basement, and made a single spacious, harmonious unit of living room, dining room and kitchen, with appropriate entry conveniences. The sleeping rooms were convenient to baths approached in a segregated, separate extended wing and the whole place was flooded with sunlight from floor to ceiling with glass.

The materials of the outside walls came inside just as appropriately and freely as those of the inside walls went outside. Intimate harmony was thus established not only in the house but with its site. *Came the "Open Plan."* The housewife herself thus planned for became the central figure in her menage and her housewifery a more charming feature (according to her ability) of her domestic establishment.

She was now more hostess "officio," operating in gracious relation to her own home, instead of being a kitchen-mechanic behind closed doors.

Nobody need care now how this thing happened. It may not be important. But if not—what is?

In addition to this new freedom with its implication of fresh responsibility for the individual homester came a technical recognition of the new materials and means by which the house was to be built. Materials were now so used as to bring out their natural beauty of character. The construction was made suitable to the appropriate use of machinery—because the machine had already become the appropriate tool of our civilization. (See essays written by myself at that time.)

To use our new materials—concrete, steel and glass, and the old ones—stone and wood—in ways that were not only expedient but beautiful was Culture now. So many new forms of treating them were devised out of the working of a new principle of building. I called it "organic."

Moreover, the house itself was so proportioned that people looked well in it as a part of them and their friends looked better in it than when they were outside it.

Thus a basic change came about in this affair of a culture for the civilization of these United States. What then took place has since floundered, flourished and faded under different names by different architects in an endless procession of expedients.

Here the original comes back to say hello to you afresh and to see if you recognize it for what it was and still is—a home for our people in the spirit in which our Democracy was conceived: the individual integrate and free in an environment of his own, appropriate to his circumstances—a life beautiful as he can make it—with her, of course.

USONIAN HOUSE AND EXHIBITION PAVILION, FIFTH AVENUE, NEW YORK.

From "The Architectural Forum," on the exhibition, Sixty Years of Living Architecture: The Work of Frank Lloyd Wright, New York, 1953: "In this 1,700 sq. ft. exhibition house lie Frank Lloyd Wright's suggestions to the average American who builds or buys a home—suggestions first made in 1900 when his houses embodying the same principles first appeared on the prairie outside Chicago. Here for the first time in the Architecture of the West the human scale in building proportion appeared with the open plan. This two-bedroom Usonian house has a simple in-line plan and is within the reach of many. Thousands of New Yorkers who walked through it experienced for the first time the design qualities Wright has talked about since the turn of the century: spaciousness and sunlight, human scale, warmth and solidity, a feeling of shelter, and a sense of the outdoors."

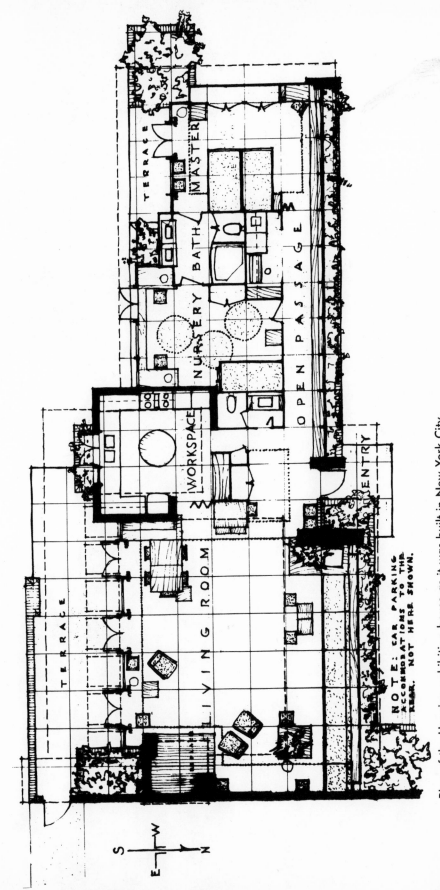

TERRACE

LIVING ROOM

WORKSPACE

NURSERY BATH MASTER

TERRACE

OPEN PASSAGE

ENTRY

NOTE: CAR PARKING ACCOMMODATIONS TO THE REAR. NOT HERE SHOWN.

Plan of the Usonian exhibition house as it was built in New York City.

S
E — W
N

Low, closed side of living room unit, as seen from kitchen, has built-in seat with storage in a deep, sheltering cove that extends across the entire living room facing the fireplace. Clerestory windows are toward the street and the neighbors, assuring natural light on all sides of the room whatever the orientation—and affording privacy. Brick wall at far end is pierced in natural block pattern.

(below) High, open side of living room, seen from entry, faces living terrace and view (walled in only because of New York City limitations). All furniture is by Frank Lloyd Wright or influenced by him including the specially designed spherical black kettle. In charge of construction: David Henken of Henken Builds, Inc., a former Wright apprentice, assisted by 14 boys of the Taliesin Fellowship. Fifteen years ago, this was about a $15,000 house.

View from terrace looking into living room. Tall glass doors extend to full height of 12' ceiling, throwing the big living room wide open to its terrace on occasion. Roof overhang is richly patterned with rhythmic openings and the ornamental dentil bands characteristic of the whole structure; a place for vines overhead.

(below) Sunlight and a sense of deep space play freely through the 26' x 32' living-dining area, giving it a sense of great repose and comfort. Interior is warm in color and alive with deep red texture of brick, a checkerboard ceiling of red oak plywood, twinkling accents of light in brass spotlight plates, repeated in the piano hinges, on tall windows, and doors, copper fillets on shelves and tables. Folding screen makes kitchen an admirable part of the whole living room unit.

A glimpse of the long gallery leading from entry to living room and bedrooms as 34 feet of storage wall alongside wall, a laundry alcove opposite. Hall lavatory-toilet is convenient to entrance and to living room (foreground).

Tall central kitchen, itself planned as a ventilating feature of the entire living room unit, around a table for assembling of meals, has a tall view window at left and a skylight above—with built-in ovens, cabinets and sideboard accommodations.

At the end of this segregation of the bedrooms is the master bedroom, secure and intimate with its rich wood finishes, dramatic spotlighting, high windows filtering sunlight through patterned shutters, belonging to the style of the whole.

BOOK TWO: 1954

INTEGRITY: IN A HOUSE

AS IN AN INDIVIDUAL

What is needed most in architecture today is the very thing that is most needed in life—Integrity. Just as it is in a human being, so integrity is the deepest quality in a building; but it is a quality not much demanded of any building since very ancient times when it was natural. It is no longer the first demand for a human being either, because "Success" is now so immediately necessary. If you are a success, people will not want to "look the gift horse in the mouth." No. But then if "success" should happen today something precious has been lost from life.

Somebody has described a man of this period as one through the memory of whom you could too easily pass your hand. Had there been true *quality* in the man the hand could not so easily pass. That quality in the memory of him would probably have been "Integrity."

In speaking of integrity in architecture, I mean much the same thing that you would mean were you speaking of an individual. Integrity is not something to be put on and taken off like a garment. Integrity is a quality *within* and *of* the man himself. So it is in a building. It cannot be changed by any other person either nor by the exterior pressures of any outward circumstances; integrity cannot change except from within because it is that in you which *is you*—and due to which you will try to live your life (as you would build your building) in the best possible way. To build a man or building from within is always difficult to do because deeper is not so easy as shallow.

Naturally should you want to really live in a way and in a place which is true to this deeper thing in you, which you honor, the house you build to live in as a home should be (so far as it is possible to make it so) integral in every sense. Integral to site, to purpose, and to you. The house would then be a home in the best sense of that word. This we seem to have forgotten if ever we learned it. Houses have become a series of anonymous boxes that go into a row on row upon row of bigger boxes either merely negative or a mass nuisance. But now the house in this interior or deeper organic sense may come alive as organic architecture.

We are now trying to bring *integrity* into building. If we succeed, we will have done a great service to our moral nature—the psyche—of our democratic society. Integrity would become more natural. Stand up for *integrity* in your building and you stand for integrity not only in the life of those who did the building but socially a reciprocal relationship is inevitable. An irresponsible, flashy, pretentious or dishonest individual would never be happy in such a house as we now call organic because of this quality of integrity. The one who will live in it will be he who will grow with living in it. So it is the "job" of any true architect to envision and make this human relationship—so far as lies in his power— a reality.

Living within a house wherein everything is genuine and har-

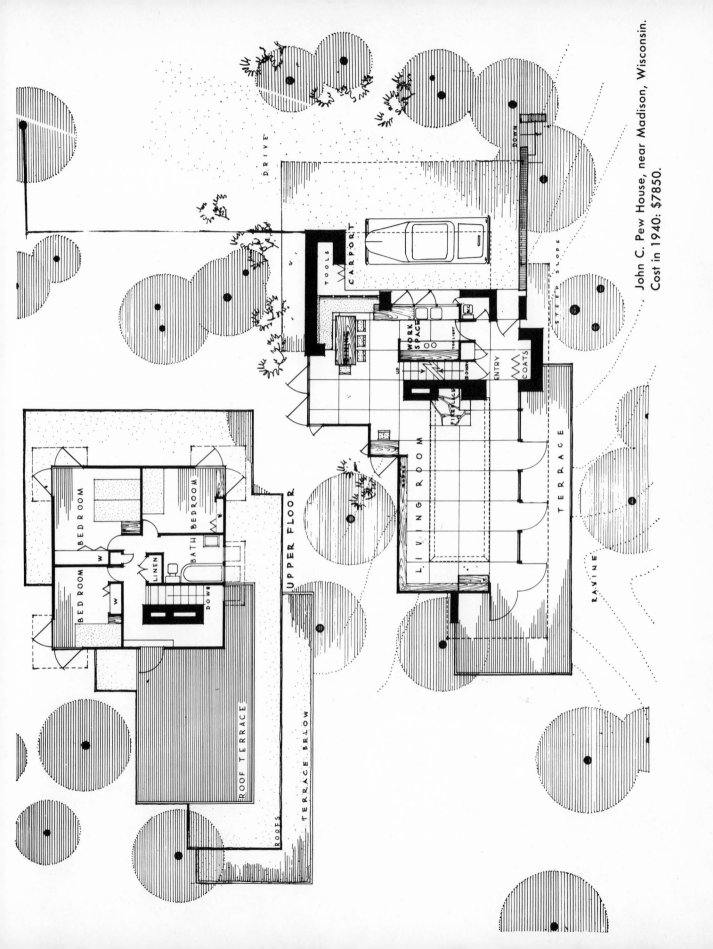

John C. Pew House, near Madison, Wisconsin.
Cost in 1940: $7850.

PEW HOUSE ON SOUTH SHORE OF LAKE MENDOTA, WISCONSIN.

monious, a new sense of freedom gives one a new sense of life—as contrasted with the usual existence in the house indiscriminately planned and where Life is *contained* within a series of confining boxes, all put within the general box. Such life is bound to be inferior to life lived in this new integrity—the Usonian Home.

In designing the Usonian house, as I have said, I have always proportioned it to the human figure in point of scale; that is, to the scale of the human figure to occupy it. The old idea in most build-

Pew House, living room. " . . . probably the only house in Madison, Wisconsin, that recognizes beautiful Lake Mendota, my boyhood lake . . . a house actually built by the Taliesin Fellowship."

ings was to make the human being feel rather insignificant—developing an inferiority complex in him if possible. The higher the ceilings were then the greater the building was. This empty grandeur was considered to be human luxury. Of course, great, high ceilings had a certain utility in those days, because of bad planning and awkward construction. (The volume of contained air was about all the air to be had without violence.)

The Usonian house, then, aims to be a *natural* performance, one that is integral to site; integral to environment; integral to the life of the inhabitants. A house integral with the nature of materials—wherein glass is used as glass, stone as stone, wood as wood—and all the elements of environment go into and throughout the house.

The Pew House is a two-story wood and stone house built of lapped cypress boards inside and out.

Into this new integrity, once there, those who live in it will take root and grow. And most of all belonging by nature to the nature of its being.

Living room, looking out over Lake Mendota.

Whether people are fully conscious of this or not, they actually derive countenance and sustenance from the "atmosphere" of the things they live in or with. They are rooted in them just as a plant is in the soil in which it is planted. For instance, we receive many letters from people who sing praises for what has happened to them as a consequence; telling us how their house has affected their lives. They now have a certain dignity and pride in their environment; they see it has a meaning or purpose which they share as a family or feel as individuals.

We all know the feeling we have when we are well-dressed and like the consciousness that results from it. It affects our conduct and you should have the same feeling regarding the home you live in. It has a salutary effect morally, to put it on a lower plane than it deserves, but there are higher results above that sure one. If you feel yourself becomingly housed, know that you are living according to the higher demands of good society, and of your own conscience, then you are free from embarrassment and not poor in spirit but rich—in the right way. I have always believed in being careful about my clothes; getting well-dressed because I could then forget all about them. That is what should happen to you with a good house that is a *home.* When you are conscious that the house is right and is honestly becoming to you, and feel you are living in it beautifully, you need no longer be concerned about it. It is no tax upon your conduct, nor a nag upon your self-respect, because it is featuring you as you like to see yourself.

Space flows uninterrupted below this two-story house lifted by stone columns at one end of hilly site.

Workspace merges into dining area.

Living room fireplace, dining table arrangement beyond.

FROM THE GROUND UP

WHERE TO BUILD

When selecting a site for your house, there is always the question of how close to the city you should be and that depends on what kind of slave you are. The best thing to do is go as far out as you can get. Avoid the suburbs—dormitory towns—by all means. Go way out into the country—what you regard as "too far"—and when others follow, as they will (if procreation keeps up), move on.

Of course it all depends on how much time you have to get there and how much time you can afford to lose, going and coming. But Decentralization is under way. You may see it everywhere. Los Angeles is a conspicuous example of it. There the powers that be are trying to hold it downtown. Robert Moses is struggling to release New York to the country. He thinks he is doing the opposite. But he isn't. New York's Moses is another kind of Moses leading his people *out* from the congestion rather than into it—leading the people from the city.

So go out with these big ferry-boats gnashing their chromium teeth at you as they come around the corner. But don't buy the huge American car with protruding corners but buy the smaller one, such as Nash has produced, and go thirty or forty miles to the gallon. A gallon of gas is not so expensive that you cannot afford to pay for the gas it takes to get pretty far from the city. The cost of transportation has been greatly decreased by way of the smaller car. In this way, decentralization has found aid, and the easier the means of egress gets to be, the further you can go out from the city.

I tried to get a congregation out of the city when we built the Unitarian Church in Wisconsin, but before it was finished, a half dozen buildings had sprung up around it. Now it is merely suburban instead of in the country. In Arizona we went twenty-six miles from the center of town to build Taliesin West; and are now there where we will soon be suburban, too. Clients have asked me: "How far should we go out, Mr. Wright?" I say: "Just ten times as far as you think you ought to go." So my suggestion would be to go just as far as you can go—and go soon and go fast.

There is only one solution, one principle, one proceeding which can rid the city of its congestion—decentralization. Go out, un-divide the division, un-subdivide the division, and then sub-divide the un-subdivision. The only answer to life today is to get back to the good ground, or rather I should say, to get forward to it, because now instead of going back, we can go foward to the ground: not the city going to the country but the country and city becoming one. We have the means to go, a means that is entirely adequate to human purposes where life is now most concerned. Because we have the automobile, we can go far and fast and when we get there, we have other machines to use—the tractor or whatever else you may want to use.

We have all the means to live free and independent, far apart—as we choose—still retaining all the social relationships and advantages we ever had, even to have them greatly multiplied. No matter if we do have houses a quarter of a mile apart. You would enjoy all that you used to enjoy when you were ten to a block, and think of the immense advantages for your children and for yourself: freedom to *use* the ground, relationship with all kinds of living growth.

There is no sense in herding any more. It went out when we got cheap and quick transportation. When we got a kind of building, too, that requires more space. The old building was a box—a fortification more or less. It was a box which could be put close to other boxes so that you could live as close together as possible—and you did. You lived so close together in houses of the Middle Ages because you had to walk to communicate. You were concentrated for safety also. So there was ground only for you to get into a huddle upon. Also, one town was liable to be attacked by townsfolk coming in from the North or from somewhere else to conquer you and take your ground away. You were forced to live compactly. Every little village in the old days was a fortress.

Today there is no such condition, nor is there ever going to be such again in our country or in any other country as far as I know. Today the threat is from the sky in the form of an atom bomb (or an even more destructive bomb), and the more you are divided and scattered, the less temptation to the bomb—the less harm the bomb could do. The more you herd now the more damage to you, as conditions now are.

Looking at it from any standpoint, decentralization is the order of this day. So go far from the city, much farther than you think you can afford. You will soon find you never can go quite far enough.

WHAT KIND OF LAND

With a small budget the best kind of land to build on is flat land. Of course, if you can get a gentle slope, the building will be more interesting, more satisfactory. But changes of ground surface make building much more expensive.

It is also cheaper to build in the South where no deep foundations or insulation are necessary, rather than in the North where summers are short and you have to prepare for them in air-conditioning a house, and for the long winters: piling up firewood, putting away food, etc., etc., etc.

But it is because of this need for resourcefulness that the man of the North has traditionally and actually conquered the man softened by the South; and then, these comforts thus won, the Northern man has himself grown soft only to be re-conquered. So it seems to go on ceaselessly.

A SUITABLE FOUNDATION

The sort of foundation that should be used for a house depends upon the place where you are going to build the house. If you are building in the desert, the best foundation is right *on* the desert. Don't dig into it and break it.

One of the best foundations I know of, suitable to many places (particularly to frost regions), was devised by the old Welsh stone-mason who put the foundations in for buildings now used by Taliesin North. Instead of digging down three and a half feet or four feet below the frost line, as was standard practice in Wisconsin, not only terribly expensive but rendering capillary attrac-

PRELIMINARY SKETCH OF LOREN POPE HOUSE, FALLS CHURCH, VIRGINIA.

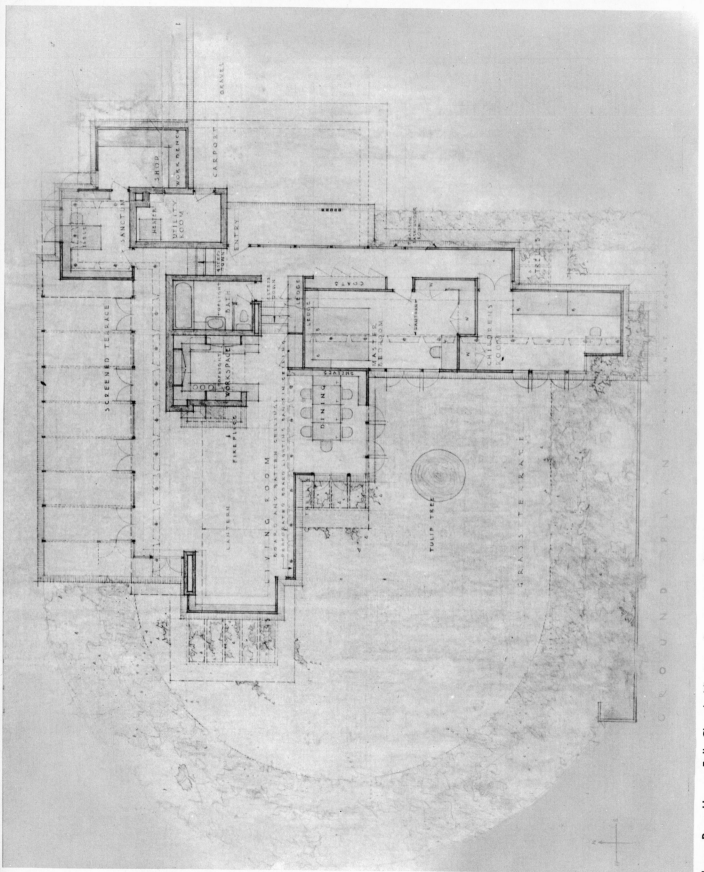

Loren Pope House, Falls Church, Virginia. Cost in 1940: $8000.

POPE HOUSE, LOOKING TOWARD SOUTHWEST.

REAR VIEW OF POPE HOUSE, FALLS CHURCH, VIRGINIA

tion a threat to the upper wall, he dug shallow trenches about sixteen inches deep and slightly pitched them to a drain. These trenches he filled with broken stone about the size of your fist. Broken stone does not clog up, and provides the drainage beneath the wall that saves it from being lifted by the frost.

I have called it the "dry wall footing," because if the wall stayed dry the frost could not affect it. In a region of deep cold to keep a building from moving it is necessary to get all water (or moisture) from underneath it. If there is no water there to freeze, the foundation cannot be lifted.

All those footings at Taliesin have been perfectly static. Ever since I discovered the dry wall footing—about 1902—I have been building houses that way. Occasionally there has been trouble getting the system authorized by building commissions. A recent encounter was with the Lake Forest Building Department of Illinois. It refused to allow the building to be so built. The Madison, Wisconsin, experts also refused to let me use the system on the hillsides above the lake. When the experts do not accept it, they will not accept the idea of saving the builders of the house many thousands of dollars. But we have in all but eight or ten cases put it through now, thereby saving the client excess waste of money below ground for no good purpose.

That type of footing, however, is not applicable to treacherous sub-soils where the problem is entirely different. For example, the Imperial Hotel was built on soil about the consistency of cheese, some eight feet thick, and a foundation for that particular soil had to be devised to bear the load of any building we wanted to build. I remembered I had bored holes with an auger on the Oak Park prairie. So I had driven into the soil a tapered pile eight feet long which punched a hole. I made tests to determine how far apart each of these piles would have to be to carry the necessary load and found that centers, two feet apart, were far enough—had they been further apart, not all of the ground would have been utilized. We punched these holes and filled them with concrete. We had to do it quickly, because, since we were almost down to water level, the water might come right up. On these tapered concrete piles we spread a thin plate of concrete slab, or beam, which gathered all these little pins in the pin cushion together and added up to enough resistance to carry the walls.

No one foundation, then, is suitable for all soils; the type of foundation used must be applicable to the particular site.

ADVANTAGES OF THE BERM-TYPE

The berm-type house, with walls of earth, is practical—a nice form of building anywhere: north, south, east or west—depending upon the soil and climate as well as the nature of the site. If your site contains a lot of boulders or rock ledges it is impossible. In the berm-type house the bulldozer comes along, pushes the dirt up against the outsides of the building as high as you want it to go and you may carry the earth banking as far around the structure as you please. Here you have good insulation—great protection from the elements; a possible economy, too, because you do not have to finish any outside below the window level. You do not have to finish the inside walls either if not so inclined. I think it an excellent form for certain regions and conditions. An actual economy and preservation of the landscape.

The drawings and plan of the Cooperative Homesteads on the following pages are of a low cost scheme for group housing. This berm-type project was begun with the assumption that the work upon the buildings would be done by the Detroit auto workers who intended to live there. It was mainly a drainage and landscape problem. But the times were such that the group could never get together with much effect on progress. Cost in 1942: $4000. The nature of the scheme is apropos to so much of the building problem in our country that it is on record here for what it may be worth.

COOPERATIVE HOMESTEADS INC
FRANK LLOYD WRIGHT ARCHITECT
DETROIT MICH

COOPERATIVE HOMESTEADS INC   DETROIT MICH

FRANK LLOYD WRIGHT ARCHITECT

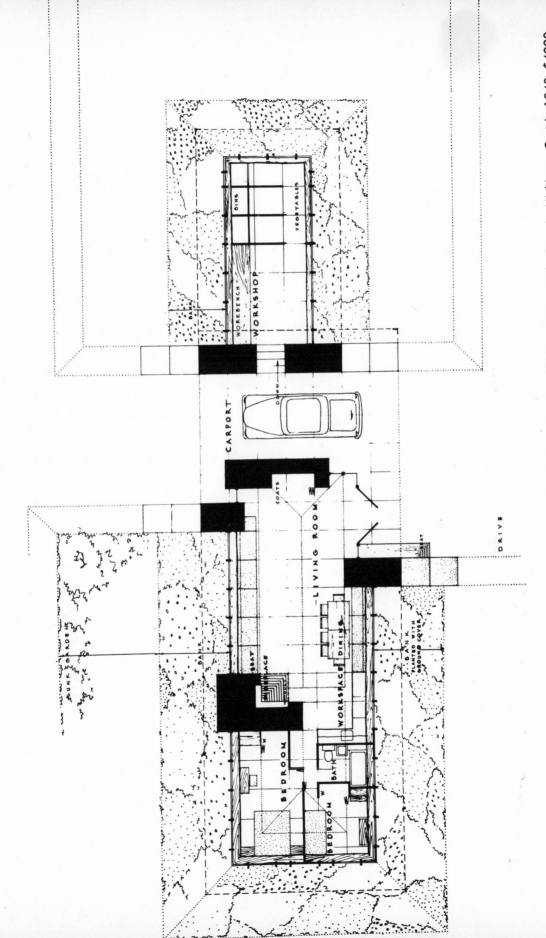

Plan of berm-house for Cooperative Homesteads, Detroit, Michigan. Cost in 1942: $4000.

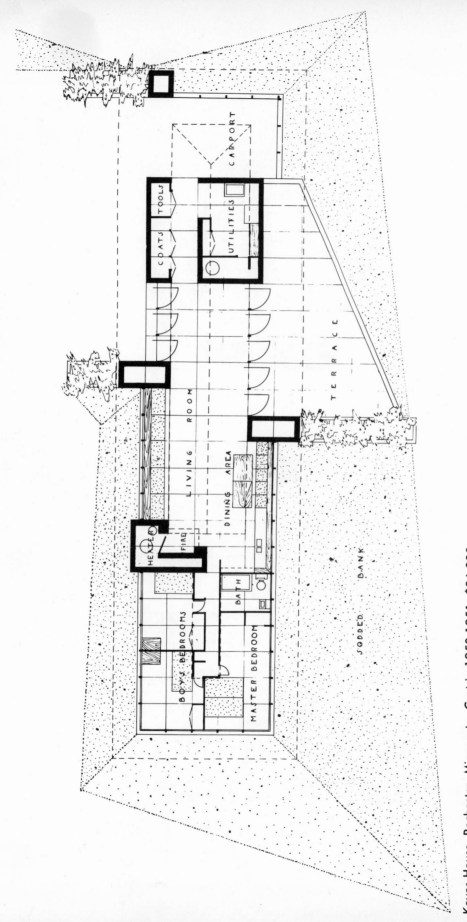

Keyes House, Rochester, Minnesota. Cost in 1950-1951: $26,000.

KEYES HOUSE, ROCHESTER, MINNESOTA.

Living room opens out on enclosed terrace.

Bedroom windows over sodded bank.

HOW TO LIGHT THE HOUSE

The best way to light a house is God's way—the natural way, as nearly as possible in the daytime and at night as nearly like the day as may be, or better.

Cities are commonly laid out north, south, east and west. This was just to save the surveyor trouble, I imagine. Anyway that happened without much thought for the human beings compelled to build homes on those lines. This inevitably results in every house having a "dark side."

Surveyors do not seem to have learned that the south is the comforter of life, the south side of the house the "living" side. Ordinarily the house should be set 30-60 to the south, well back on its site so that every room in the house might have sunlight some time in the day. If, however, owing to the surveyor the house must face square north, we always place the clerestory (which serves as a lantern) to the south so that no house need lack sunlight. It is a somewhat expensive way to overcome the surveyor's ruse.

THE GREAT LUMINARY

Proper orientation of the house, then, is the first condition of the lighting of that house; and artificial lighting is nearly as important as daylight. Day lighting can be beautifully managed by the architect if he has a feeling for the course of the sun as it goes from east to west and at the inevitable angle to the south. The sun is the great luminary of all life. It should serve as such in the building of any house. There is, however, the danger of taking "light" too far and leaving you, "the inmate," defenseless in a glass cage

—which is somewhat silly. You must control light in the planning of your home so that light most naturally serves your needs without too much artificial production and consequent control—putting light in only to block it out.

As for all artificial lighting, it too should be integral part of the house—be as near daylighting as possible. In 1893, I began to get rid of the bare light-bulb and have ever since been concealing it on interior decks or placing it in recesses in such a way that it comes from the building itself; the effect should be that it comes from the same source as natural light. Sometimes we light the grounds about the house putting outside light so that it lights the interior of the rooms.

Wiring for lights, as piping for plumbing and heating, should not show all over the house unless by special design—any more than you would have organs of your body on the outside of your skin. Lighting fixtures should (as should all others) be absorbed *in* the structure, so that their office is *of* the structure. All this after the building has been properly orientated.

STEEL AND GLASS

There is much new good in houses being built today and chiefly on account of the new freedoms afforded organic architecture by the uses of steel and glass; miraculous materials. As a result of these space is now freer, wider spans are easier; therefore more open spaces, made possible owing to steel in tension, and a closer relation to nature (environment) owing to the use of glass. These materials, everywhere to be seen now, are enabling building to go in varied directions with more ease; to go beyond the traditional constraint of the box with economy.

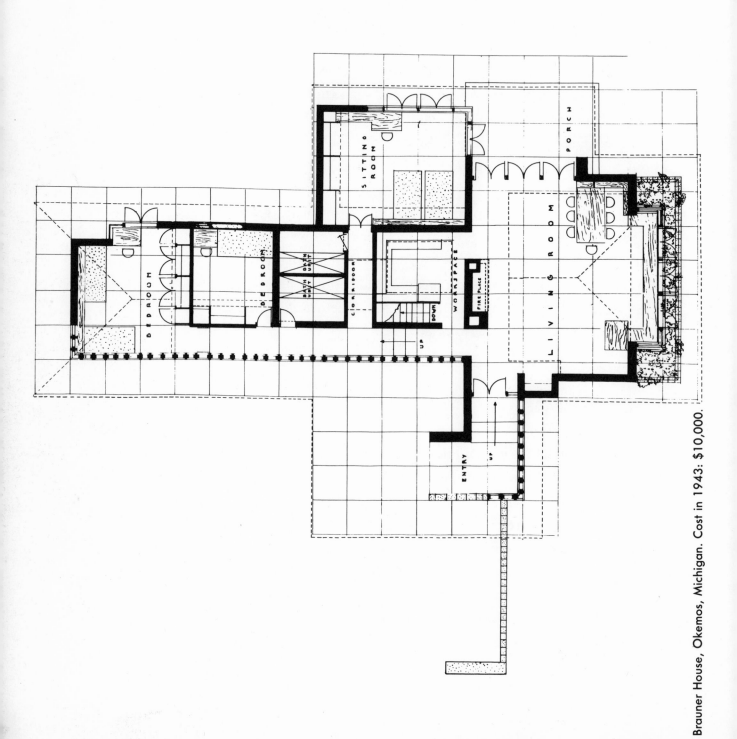

SITTING ROOM

PORCH

BEDROOM

BATH UNIT · BATH UNIT

CORRIDOR

DOWN

WORKSPACE

FIRE PLACE

LIVING ROOM

BEDROOM

UP

ENTRY

UP

Brauner House, Okemos, Michigan. Cost in 1943: $10,000.

BRAUNER HOUSE, OKEMOS, MICHIGAN. LIVING ROOM OPENS OUT ON TWO SIDES. CARPORT AT LEFT.

THE BASEMENT

A house should—ordinarily—not have a basement. In spite of everything you may do, a basement is a noisome, gaseous damp place. From it come damp atmospheres and unhealthful conditions. Because people rarely go there—and certainly not to live there—it is almost always sure to be an ugly place. The family tendency is to throw things into it, leave them there and forget them. It usually becomes—as it became when I began to build—a great, furtive underground for the house in order to enable the occupants to live in it disreputably. Also, so many good housewives, even their lords and masters, used to tumble downstairs into the basement and go on insurance for some time, if not make it all immediately collectible.

Another objection to the basement is that it is relatively expensive. It has to be some six to eight feet below grade and so you have to get big digging going. It is a great inhibition in any building because you must construct a floor over it and the space it provides you with is, as I have said, usually disreputably occupied.

Of course, a basement often is a certain convenience, but these conveniences can now be supplied otherwise. Mechanical equipment is now so compact and good-looking. So we decided to eliminate it wherever possible and provide for its equivalent up on the ground level with modern equipment.

INSULATION AND HEATING

In either a very cold or a very hot climate, the overhead is where insulation should occur in any building. There you can spend money for insulation with very good effect, whereas the insulation of the walls and the air space within the walls becomes less and less important. With modern systems of air conditioning and heating you can manage almost any condition.

But the best insulation for a roof and walls in a hot climate is nearly the same as the best insulation for a roof and walls in a cold region. Resistance to heat in a building is much the same as resistance to cold, although of course the exact specifications should vary according to circumstances. In a warm region it is important that the overhead not get overheated. You have to use a very tough cover for roof insulation or the sun will take the life out of it quickly. We have never found a roofing that lasts as long as we would like in a hot climate like the desert—but a white-top is economical partly because white, of course, reflects heat rather than absorbs it.

But in a cold climate like southern Wisconsin the real basis for purposeful insulation is floor heating. When you have the floor warm—heat by gravity—insulation of the walls becomes comparatively insignificant. You may open the windows in cold weather and still be comfortable, because, if your feet are warm and you sit warm, you are warm. In this case overhead insulation is extremely important: heat rises and if it finds a place overhead where it can be cooled off and dropped, you have to continuously supply a lot of heat. If, however, the overhead is reasonably defensive against cold, you can heat your house very economically, more so than by any other system.

On the other hand, snow is the best kind of insulation. You do not have to buy it. In northern climates you can see how well a house is insulated by noticing how quickly the snow melts off the roof. If the snow stays for some time, the roof is pretty well insulated. If you get insulation up to a certain point, snow will come and give you more. To hold snow on the roof is always a good, wise provision and a good argument for a flat roof. I have seen people shovelling snow off the roof and I never could understand why—unless the snow was creating a load that the roof could not bear or the roof was steep and the snow load might slide down and injure someone or something.

THE KIND OF ROOF

Now the *shape* of roof—whether a shed roof, a hip roof or a flat roof—depends in part on expediency and in part on your personal taste or knowledge as to what is appropriate in the circumstances.

One of the advantages of the sloping roof is that it gives you a sense of spaciousness inside, a sense of overhead uplift which I often feel to be very good. The flat roof also has advantages in construction. It is easy to do, of course. But with the flat roof, you must devise ways and means of getting rid of the water. One way to do this is to build, on top of the flat, a slight pitch to the eaves. This may be done by "furring." There are various ways of getting water off a flat roof. But it must be done.

The cheapest roof, however, is the shed roof—the roof sloping one way, more or less. There you get more for your money than you can get from any other form of roof. There is no water problem with a shed roof because the water goes down to the lower side and drops away. With a hip roof the water runs two ways into a natural valley, so there is not much problem there either.

Suitable to flat roof construction in many locations is the flat roof covered with a body of good earth—what I call the "berm type" roof. On top of the building there will be—say—about sixteen inches of good fertile earth in which may be planted grass or whatever you please to plant. There is the most natural insulation that can be devised. Probably the cheapest. Always I like the feeling you have when beneath it. The house I will build for my son, Llewellyn, in Virginia has a flat roof with earth to be placed on top.

I have also sometimes pitched roofs from high on the sides to low in the center. You can do with a roof almost anything you like. But the type of roof you choose must not only deal with the elements in your region but be appropriate to the circumstances, according to your personal preference—perhaps.

THE ATTIC

Why waste good livable space with an attic any more than with a basement? And never plan waste space in a house with the idea of eventually converting it into rooms. A house that is planned for a lot of problematical space or space unused to be used some other day is not likely to be a well-planned house. In fact, if you deliberately planned waste space, the architect would be wasted, the people in the house would be wasted. Everything would probably go to waste.

If, however, in future you are going to need more room for more children and you wish to provide that room it need not be waste space if properly conceived. But the attic, now, should always come *into* the house to beautify it. Sunlight otherwise impossible may be got into the house through the attic by way of what we call a lantern or clerestory. And that should also give you the sense of lift and beauty that comes in so many of our plans at this time.

We *use* all "waste" space: make it part of the house; make it so beautiful that as waste space it is inconceivable. It is something

Detail. Clerestory for penthouse study on upper floor of Raymond Carlson House, Phoenix, Ariz.

161

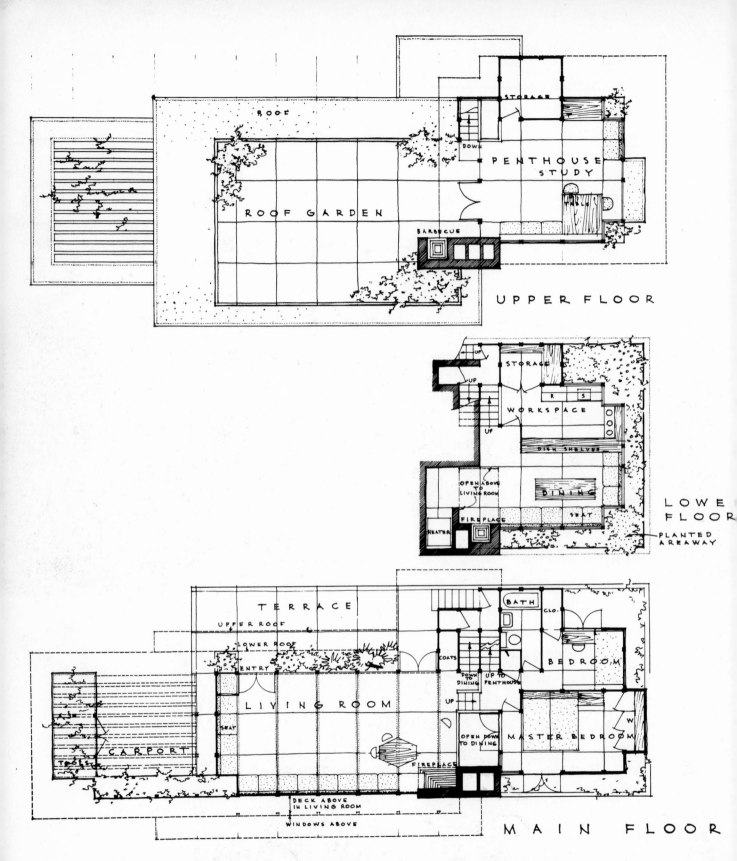

ROOF

ROOF GARDEN

STORAGE

DOWN

PENTHOUSE
STUDY

TABLE

BARBECUE

UPPER FLOOR

UP

UP

STORAGE

R   S

WORKSPACE

DISH SHELVES

UP

OPEN ABOVE
TO
LIVING ROOM

DINING

SEAT

FIREPLACE

HEATER

PLANTED
AREAWAY

LOWER
FLOOR

TERRACE

UPPER ROOF

LOWER ROOF

ENTRY

COATS

BATH

CLO.

BEDROOM

LIVING ROOM

DOWN
TO
DINING

UP TO
PENTHOUSE

UP

SEAT

OPEN DOWN
TO DINING

MASTER BEDROOM

W

CARPORT

TOOLS

FIREPLACE

DECK ABOVE
IN LIVING ROOM

WINDOWS ABOVE

MAIN FLOOR

Raymond Carlson House, Phoenix, Arizona. Cost in 1951: $16,000.

RAYMOND CARLSON HOUSE, PHOENIX, ARIZONA. VIEW TOWARD SOUTHEAST.

View from workspace through shelves to dining area, right. Planted areaway around all three sides.

RAYMOND CARLSON HOUSE, PHOENIX, ARIZONA: VIEW FROM THE EAST.

like the little boy eating an apple, and another little boy ranges up alongside and wants to know if he can have the core, but the apple-eater says—"Sorry, there ain't gonna be no core."

SIZE OF KITCHEN

In the Usonian house the size of the kitchen depends largely on the home-maker's personal preference. Some homesters like to get a lot of exercise in the homestead—walking from place to place. Some women want things on ball bearings. Some don't want to bend over; they like to stand up when they work: for them we put everything high: ovens up in the wall, etc. Women who do not mind bending over like things more compact; they do not want to waste their substance going to and fro. For them we put things on ball bearings as you may easily do now that modern gadgetry is so well designed.

So we like to make kitchens small, and put things on ball bearings. We have more money to spend on spaciousness for the rest of the house. Sometimes we are caught making a kitchen too small, and then the woman of the house comes in and asks us to make it bigger; sometimes they get this but sometimes they do not—it depends on the good proportions of the design as a whole.

But I believe in having a kitchen featured as the work space in the Usonian house and a becoming part of the living room—a welcome feature. Back in farm days there was but one big living room, a stove in it, and Ma was there cooking—looking after the children and talking to Pa—dogs and cats and tobacco smoke too —all gemütlich if all was orderly, but it seldom was; and the children were there playing around. It created a certain atmosphere of a domestic nature which had charm and which is not, I think, a good thing to lose altogether. Consequently, in the Usonian plan the kitchen was called "workspace" and identified largely with the living room. As a matter of fact, it became an alcove of the living room but higher for good ventilation and spaciousness.

The kitchen being one of the places where smells originated, we made that the ventilating flue of the whole house by carrying it up higher than the living room. All the air from the surrounding house was thus drawn up through the kitchen itself. You might have liver and onions for dinner and never know it in the living room, until it was served to you at the table. The same is true of other smells and conditions in the way the bathrooms were made. We were never by this means able to eliminate noise. So in a Usonian house a needlessly noisy kitchen is a bad thing.

Everything in the Usonian kitchen should be (as it may so easily be) modern and attractive as such. Because it is incorporated into the living room, the kitchen (workspace) should be just as charming to be in or look at as the living room—perhaps more so. When we built the Usonian house in the New York Exhibition (fall of 1953) the kitchen was a delightful little place to look at, no less so as a "work place."

THE CLIENT AND THE HOUSE

The needs and demands of the average client should affect every feature of a house but only insofar as the clients do manifest intelligence instead of exert mere personal idiosyncrasy. This manifestation of intelligence is not so rare. Yet when a man has "made his money"—is therefore a "success"—he then thinks, because of this "success," that he can tell you, or anybody else, all about things of which he really knows nothing at all—a house in particular. His success as a maker-of-money makes him a universal expert. So he begins to exercise his idiosyncrasies as this universal expert.

But I've really had little enough trouble with good businessmen or their wives. They *do* have what we call "common sense." A man does have to have common sense to make any sort of fortune in this country dedicated to ruthless competition—and you can usually explain the subtle inner nature of things to a man of good sense who has never thought about them—but must now go in for them.

But, the wife? Well, too often she is quite another matter, having made him what he is today. Although the wives we encounter are so often far wiser in this affair of home making than their husbands. The peripatetic marriage is the enemy of good architecture—as a matter of course.

EXPANDING FOR GROWING FAMILY

A Usonian house if built for a young couple, can, without deformity, be expanded, later, for the needs of a growing family. As you see from the plans, Usonian houses are shaped like polliwogs—a house with a shorter or longer tail. The body of the polliwog is the living room and the adjoining kitchen—or work space—and the whole Usonian concentration of conveniences. From there it starts out, with a tail: in the proper direction, say, one bedroom, two bedrooms, three, four, five, six bedrooms long; provision between each two rooms for a convenient bathroom. We sometimes separate this tail from the living room wing with a loggia—for quiet, etc.; especially grace.

The size of the polliwog's tail depends on the number of children and the size of the family budget. If the tail gets too long, it may curve like a centipede. Or you might break it, make it angular. The wing can go on for as many children as you can afford to put in it. A good Usonian house seems to be no less but more adapted to be an ideal breeding stable than the box.

CHILDREN'S ROOMS

People who have many children want to build a house usually, but do not have enough money to do justice to the children. As a rule, they do not have *any* on account of the children. But they keep on having children just the same no matter what else they may do or not do. So you see their architect has to tuck the extra children in somehow; and the idea seems to be to give them the smallest possible sleeping space with double deckers but to try also to give them a playroom. If possible this should be apart from sleeping quarters. Or build a separate section entirely for progeny.

For the children's bedrooms, then, we introduced the double-decker bed. We put two children in a small room next to a bath—two children high is the limit in most of our houses. But you could put in a third. The boys and girls still have to be separated, for some mysterious reason. So the compact three-bedroom house is about the minimum now.

The playroom is planned as part outdoors and part indoors and so gives children a little liberty for play, etc. Usually, of course, they now play in the living room and the house is a bedlam. Everything loose is likely to be turned inside out or upside down, and there is not much use trying to do anything about them at that. Building a house for the average family (children and their adults) is a pretty rough extravaganza. Either the children get left or must get spanked into place, else they have the whole house and the grown-ups do what they can do to make themselves as comfortable as they may be able.

It is more important for the child to live in an appropriate, well-considered home development than it is for the grown-ups, because the grown-ups are halfway through and consequently do not have so much to lose or gain from the home atmosphere. The child, however, is a beginning; he has the whole way to go and he may go a lot further in the course of time than Pa and Ma ever had a chance to go. But after forty—even thirty-five—the home is not so important for the parents as for the child, as the case may be, although they leave soon for homes of their own. The Catholics say, "Give me a child up to the age of seven, and who cares who takes the child after that." This is because it is in childhood that impressions become most indelible.

For these and many unmentioned reasons it is peculiarly important that a child should grow up in building conditions that are harmonious, live in an atmosphere that contributes to serenity and wellbeing and to the consciousness of those things which are more excellent, in childhood. What a pity that parents have children so fast, so inconsiderately, that their architect must put them into little cells, double-decker them, and shove them off into the tail of the house where life becomes one certain round of washing diapers.

FURNISHINGS

Rugs, draperies and furnishings that are suitable for a Usonian house are those, too, that are organic in character; that is, textures and patterns that sympathize in their own design and construction with the design and construction of the particular house they occupy and embellish (or befoul). A mobile, for instance, should be composed of the design elements of the room it hangs in.

Out of the nature of the materials used in building a house come these new effects. The "effect" is not all that the artist-architect gives you. He not only sees more or less clearly the nature of the materials but, in his own trained imagination and by virtue of his own feeling, he qualifies it all as a whole. You can only choose the result that is sympathetic to you.

The range of choice is growing wider now. But it is extraordinary still to see how the manufacturer is trying to burn the candle at both ends, still hanging on to the old William Morris era and old rococo fabrics. You may—at your own peril—get L'art Nouveaux, rococo, Morris, ancient and modern in the same store for the same purpose for the same price.

CHAIRS

My early approach to the chair was something between contempt and a desperation. Because I believe sitting to be in itself an unfortunate necessity not quite elegant yet, I do not yet believe in any such thing as a "natural" chair for an unnatural posture. The only attractive posture of relaxation is that of reclining. So I think the ideal chair is one which would allow the would-be "sitter" to gracefully recline. Even the newest market chairs are the usual machines-for-sitting. Now I do not know if whatever God may be ever intended you or me to fold up on one of these—but, if so, let's say that fold-up or double-up ought to make you look more graceful. It ought to look as though it were intended for you to look and be just that.

We now build well-upholstered benches and seats in our houses,

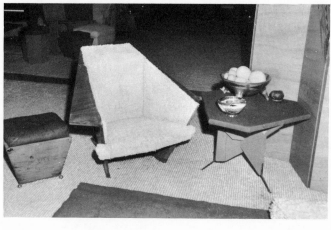

trying to make them all part of the building. But still you must bring in and pull up the casual chair. There are many kinds of

"pull-up" chairs to perch upon—lightly. They're more easy. They're
light. But the big chair wherein you may fold up and go to sleep
reading a newspaper (all that kind of thing) is still difficult. I have
done the best I could with this "living room chair" but, of course,
you have to call for somebody to help you move it. All my life my

legs have been banged up somewhere by the chairs I have designed. But we are accomplishing it now. Someday it will be well done. But it will not have metal spider-legs nor look the way most of the steel furniture these days looks to me. No—it will not be a case of "Little Miss Muffet sat on her tuffet, eating of curds and whey, when up beside her came a great black spider and frightened Miss Muffet away." I am for "Little Miss Muffet" frightened by the spider—away.

Yet every chair must eventually be designed for the building it is to be used in. Organic architecture calls for this chair which will not look like an apparatus but instead be seen as a gracious fea-

Dining chairs.
Taliesin West.

ture of its environment which can only be the building itself. So the stuffed-box-for-sitting-in is not much better than the machine-for-setting-it-in.

No doubt most practical sitters are troubled by these chairs, too. Finding a good comfortable chair in which to place one's trunk is never quite easy and so most sitting to date still lacks dignity and repose. But it is possible now to design a chair in which any sitter is compelled to look comfortable whether he is so or not.

And there is no reason why he, or she, should not be comfortable in mind as well as body folded up or down.

When the house-interior absorbs the chair as in perfect harmony, then we will have achieved not so minor a symptom of a culture of our own.

Corner of living room, Taliesin West.

PAINT

In organic architecture there is little or no room for appliqué of any kind. I have never been fond of paints or of wallpaper or anything which must be applied *to* other things as a surface. If you can put something by skill *on* the thing that becomes part *of* it and still have that thing retain its *original character* that may be good. But when you gloss it over, lose its nature—enamel it, and so change the character of its natural expression, you have committed a violation according to the ideals of organic architecture. We use nothing applied which tends to eliminate the true character of what is beneath, or which may become a substitute for whatever that may be. Wood is wood, concrete is concrete, stone is stone. We like to have whatever we choose to use demonstrate the beauty of its own character, as itself.

The only treatment we aim to give to any material is to preserve it pretty much as it *is*. A strange fallacy has developed that to paint wood preserves it. The reverse is true. Wood must breathe just as you must breathe. When you seal wood off from this innate need to breathe, you have not lengthened its life at all, you have done just the opposite. Merely staining wood is one thing; painting is quite another. When you coat anything in the way of a natural material you are likely to shorten its life, not preserve it.

AIR CONDITIONING?

To me air conditioning is a dangerous circumstance. The extreme changes in temperature that tear down a building also tear down the human body. Building is difficult in a temperate zone, where you have extreme heat and extreme cold. For instance —the boards in the ceiling over my bedroom at Taliesin West, overheated during the day, begin to pull and crack and miniature explosions occur at about three o'clock in the cool of the morning. Owing to changes of temperature nothing in construction is ever completely still.

The human body, although more flexible, is framed and constructed upon much the same principles as a building. I can sit in my shirt sleeves at eighty degrees, or seventy-five, and be cool;

then go outside to 118 degrees, take a guarded breath or two around and soon get accustomed to the change. The human body is able continually to adjust itself—to and fro. But if you carry these contrasts too far too often, when you are cooled the heat becomes more unendurable; it becomes hotter and hotter outside as you get cooler and cooler inside. Finally, Nature will give up. She will just say for you, "Well, what's the use?" Even Nature can't please everybody all the time.

So air conditioning has to be done with a good deal of intelligent care. The less the degree of temperature difference you live in, the better for your constitutional welfare. If one may have air and feel the current of air moving in on one's face and hands and feet one can take almost any degree of heat. But as for myself if I feel close *and* hot, I cannot well take it. Neither can anybody else, I believe.

So, in a very hot climate, the way to deal with air conditioning best would be to have a thorough protection overhead and the rest of the building as open to the breezes as it possibly can be made.

TALIESIN WEST, PARADISE VALLEY, NEAR PHOENIX, ARIZONA.

On the desert slopes at Taliesin West there is always a breeze. But when we first went there, and spent a summer in town, I had to wrap myself in wet sheets to get to sleep. Being a man from the North, I was unaccustomed to such heat as came from living in a bake-oven. But if I lived there all year round—and could get air by breezes—I would soon get accustomed to it.

Another way of dealing with air conditioning in a humid, hot climate is the "fireplace" as I devised it for a house in tropical Acapulco, Mexico. In this "fireplace" the air came down the flue instead of going out, and the hearth was a pool of cool water as artificial rain poured down the chimney and the pool was cooled by one of the devices designed for air conditioning. You could sit around the "fireplace" and be especially cool but the rooms were each cooled. The chimney now did not stick up much above the roof—it was just rounded up to keep the water from running in— just a low little exuberance on the roof.

Even in cold climates air conditioning has now caught on because the aim now is to maintain the degree of humidity for comfort

TALIESIN NORTH, SPRING GREEN, WISCONSIN

within, no matter what is going on outside. I do not much believe in that. I think it far better to go *with* the natural climate than try to fix a special artificial climate of your own. Climate means something to man. It means something in relation to one's life in it. Nature makes the body flexible and so the life of the individual invariably becomes adapted to environment and circumstance. The color and texture of the human skin, for an example—dark or bright—is a climatic adaptation—nothing else. Climate makes the human skin. The further north you go, the more bleached the hair and the whiter the skin, even the eyes; everything becomes pallid. The further south, the darker everything gets. It is climatic condition that does the protective coloring. I doubt that you can ignore climate completely, by reversal make a climate of your own and get away with it without harm to yourself.

THE CONTRACTOR

In choosing a contractor, the only way to judge him is to look carefully into his previous work. You should be able to tell fairly well from what he has done what he may do.

Dankmar Adler—the old Chief—used to say that he would rather give work to a crook who does know how to build than to an honest man who does not know how to build. He had this to say about that: "I can police a crook, but if a man doesn't know good work, how am I to get it out of him?" Remember also what Shakespeare said about one's not being able to make a silk purse out of a sow's ear?

GRAMMAR: THE HOUSE AS A WORK OF ART

Every house worth considering as a work of art must have a grammar of its own. "Grammar," in this sense, means the same thing in any construction—whether it be of words or of stone or wood. It is the shape-relationship between the various elements that enter into the constitution of the thing. The "grammar" of the house is its manifest articulation of all its parts. This will be the "speech" it uses. To be achieved, construction must be grammatical.

Your limitations of feeling about what you are doing, your choice of materials for the doing (and your budget of course) determine largely what grammar your building will use. It is largely inhibited (or expanded) by the amount of money you have to spend, a feature only of the latitude you have. When the chosen grammar is finally adopted (you go almost indefinitely with it into everything you do) walls, ceilings, furniture, etc., become inspired by it. Everything has a related articulation in relation to the whole and all belongs together; looks well together because all together are speaking the same language. If one part of your house spoke Choctaw, another French, another English, and another some sort of gibberish, you would have what you mostly have now—not a very beautiful result. Thus, when you do adopt the "grammar" of your house—it will be the way the house is to be "spoken," "uttered." You must be consistently grammatical for it to be understood as a work of Art.

Consistency in grammar is therefore the property—solely—of a well-developed artist-architect. Without that property of the artist-architect not much can be done about your abode as a work

D W E L L I N G   F O R   M R   A

F   R   A   N

of Art. Grammar is no property for the usual owner or the occupant of the house. But the man who designs the house must, inevitably, speak a consistent thought-language in his design. It properly may be and should be a language of his own if appropriate. If he has no language, so no grammar, of his own, he must adopt one; he will speak some language or other whether he so chooses or not. It will usually be some kind of argot.

MRS KENNETH LAURENT
ROCKFORD, ILLINOIS
LLOYD WRIGHT ARCHITECT

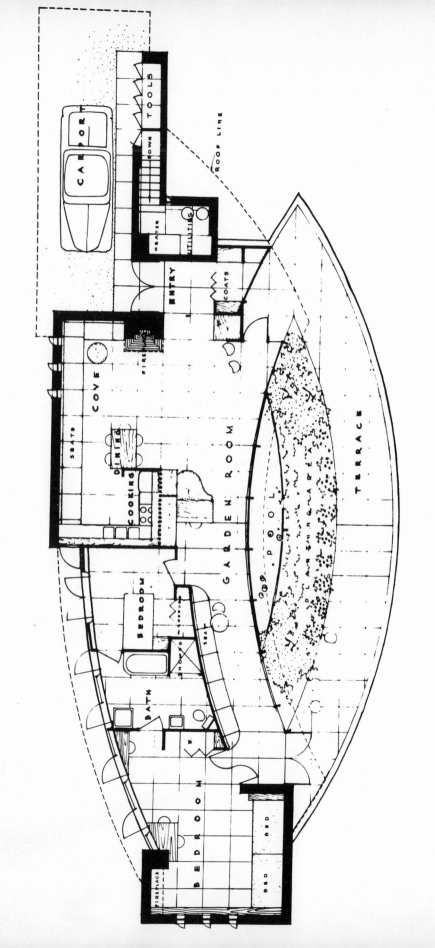

Kenneth Laurent House, Rockford, Illinois. Cost in 1952: $27,000.

LAURENT HOUSE, ROCKFORD, ILLINOIS. GARDEN ROOM OPENS OUT ON CURVED TERRACE.

THE ARCHITECT OF THE FUTURE

The first thing to do to get a Usonian house is to go to a Usonian architect! That is to say, go to some architect who has been trained from the ground up in consistent organic construction and has lived in it as a natural circumstance. He may have absorbed it only intellectually. But through the pores of his skin, his soul becomes awakened and aware of it (he will say instinctively) by his own experience.

I doubt that this affair can be *taught* to anyone. It does not come from a university with some degree or other. You cannot get it from books alone and certainly no conditioned Harvard man would be likely to have it. Harvard seems degraded to believe in the work of the committee-meeting instead of the inspired individual. But I know you can never get it through any form of collectivism. A true work of art must be induced as inspiration and cannot be induced or inspired through "teamwork." So it will not come through communism or fascism or any ism—only as slow growth by way of Democracy.

I doubt if there is much hope for the present generation's ever learning to discriminate surely between what makes a building good or what it is that makes a bad one. Hope lies within the next generation now in high school.

It is necessary for the child to grow up in an atmosphere conducive to the absorption of true esthetic values. It is necessary to study building as a kind of doing called Architecture. Not merely is Architecture made at the drafting board, but Architecture in all of its aspects is to be studied as environment, as the nature of materials to be used, as the forms and proportions of Nature itself in all her forms—sequences and consequences. Nature is the great teacher—man can only receive and respond to her teaching.

IT IS VALIANT TO BE SIMPLE

One of the essential characteristics of organic architecture is a natural simplicity. I don't mean the side of a barn door. Plainness, although simple, is not what I mean by simplicity. Simplicity is a clean, direct expression of that essential quality of the thing which is in the nature of the thing itself. The innate or organic pattern of the form of anything is that form which is thus truly *simple*. Cultivation seems to go against simplicity in the flower, as it does much the same thing in human life with the human being.

As we live and as we are, Simplicity—with a capital "S"—is difficult to comprehend nowadays. We are no longer truly simple. We no longer live in simple terms, in simple times or places. Life is a more complex struggle now. It is now valiant to be simple; a courageous thing to even want to be simple. It is a spiritual thing to comprehend what simplicity means.

In attempting to arrive at definitions of these matters, we invariably get into the spirit. The head alone cannot do enough. We have overrated what the head can do, consequently we now are confused and in a dangerous situation where our future is concerned. We have given up those things that are leading lights to the spirit of man; they are unfortunately no longer sufficiently important to us for us to pay for them what they cost.

This architecture we call organic is an architecture upon which true American society will eventually be based if we survive at all. An architecture upon and within which the common man is given freedom to realize his potentialities as an individual—himself unique, creative, free.

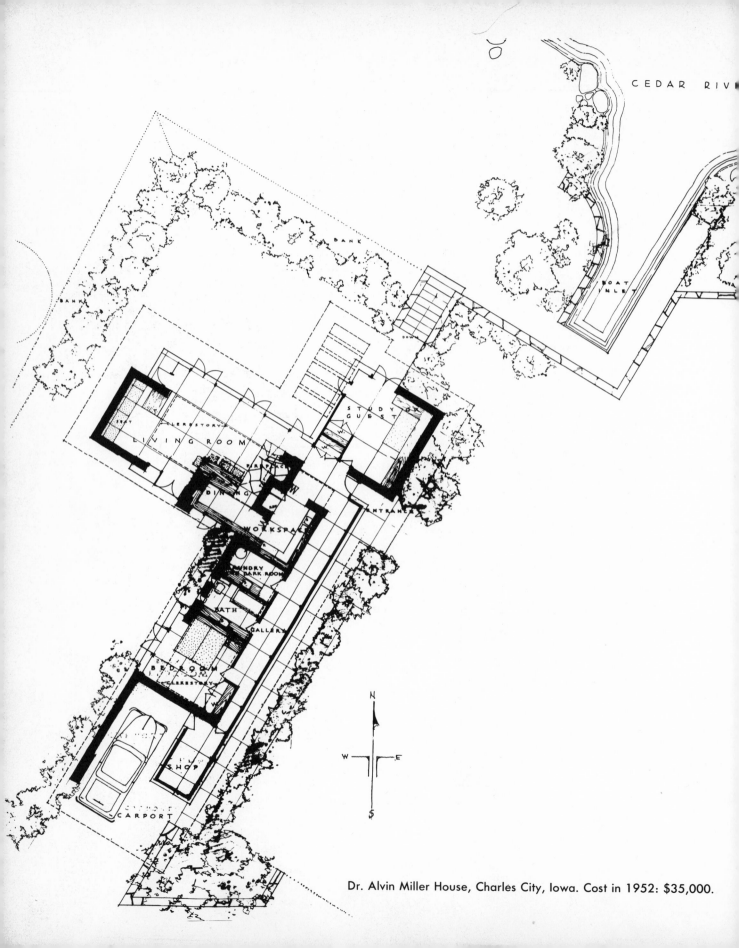

CEDAR RIVER

BANK

BANK

BANK

BOAT INLET

LIVING ROOM

STUDY OR GUEST

FIREPLACE

DINING

WORKSPACE

LAUNDRY & DARK ROOM

ENTRANCE

BATH

GALLERY

BEDROOM

CLERESTORY

SHOP

CARPORT

N
W — E
S

Dr. Alvin Miller House, Charles City, Iowa. Cost in 1952: $35,000.

MILLER HOUSE AND GARDEN, VIEW FROM RIVER BANK, LOOKING TOWARD LIVING ROOM.

View toward river taken from under broad overhanging trellis near guest study.

View toward south through glazed doors to guest wing at left, living room at right.

Living room seen from workspace. Glazed doors open on to river terrace and view of river. Dining table in foreground center.

View from entry toward workspace, showing folding board screen and workspace cabinets. Interior woodwork is cypress.

(left) Living room seen from fireplace. The clerestory spreads diffused light through room and provides ventilation in summer. Carpets are soft gold. Concrete floors are colored soft gold and waxed.

View toward northeast, past entry door and wall of guest room; river terrace above Cedar River in background.

Southeast view from entrance court. Masonry is native limestone. Cement plaster screen wall along gallery shields house from street. Flat roofs with cypress facia.

THE "USONIAN AUTOMATIC"

We are often asked how a young couple, with a limited budget, can afford to build a house designed on these basic principles of organic architecture. What couple does not have a limited budget? It is within limitations that we have to work in designing houses for the upper middle third of the democratic strata in our country. Our clients come from that strata. We are often asked: "Will you build a house for us for $15,000;" or "Will you build us a house for $25,000;" sometimes for $75,000 or even $200,000.

The other day someone came with $250,000. He embarrassed me. Very wealthy people usually go to some fashionable architect, not to a known radical who is never fashionable if he can help it.

REDUCING THE COSTS

How then, you may ask, can people with even more limited means experience the liberation, the sense of freedom that comes with true architecture? This problem will probably always exist in one direction or another. But we have gone far in solving this generic problem by the natural concrete block house we call the "Usonian Automatic." This Usonian house incorporates innovations which reduce most of the heavier building costs, labor in particular. The earlier verisions of these concrete block houses built in Los Angeles about 1921-24 may also be seen in the Arizona-Biltmore cottages. The Millard house in Pasadena was first; then the Storer and Freeman and last—the Ennis house in Los Angeles. Among recent examples are the Adelman cottage and Pieper cottage in Phoenix, Arizona.

With the limited budget of a G. I. you cannot pay a plasterer, mason, bricklayer, carpenter, etc., twenty-nine dollars a day (and at that never be sure whether the work is done well). To build a low cost house you must eliminate, so far as possible, the use of skilled labor, now so expensive. The Usonian Automatic house therefore is built of shells made up of pre-cast concrete blocks about 1′ 0″ x 2′ 0″ or larger and so designed that, grooved as they are on their edges, they can be made and also set up with small steel horizontal and vertical reinforcing rods in the joints, by the owners themselves, each course being grouted (poured) as it is laid upon the one beneath; the rods meantime projecting above for the next course.

HOW THE "USONIAN AUTOMATIC" IS BUILT

The Usonian Automatic system is capable of infinite modifications of form, pattern and application, and to any extent. The original blocks are made on the site by ramming concrete into

wood or metal wrap-around forms, with one outside face (which

may be patterned), and one rear or inside face, generally coffered, for lightness.

All edges of the blocks, having a semi-circular groove (vertically and horizontally), admit the steel rods. When blocks are placed, edges closely adjoining, cylindrical hollow spaces are formed between them in which the light steel "pencil" rods are set and into which semi-liquid Portland cement grout is poured.

Walls may be either *single* (one layer of blocks), the coffered back-face forming the interior wall surface, or *double* with two layers of blocks, with an interior insulating air space between.

Ordinarily the procedure of erection of walls is as follows:

a) Vertical reinforcing bars or dowels are set on unit intervals in slab or in footing which is to receive the block wall-construction.

b) The blocks are set between these rods so that one vertical rod falls in the round cylindrical groove between each two blocks.

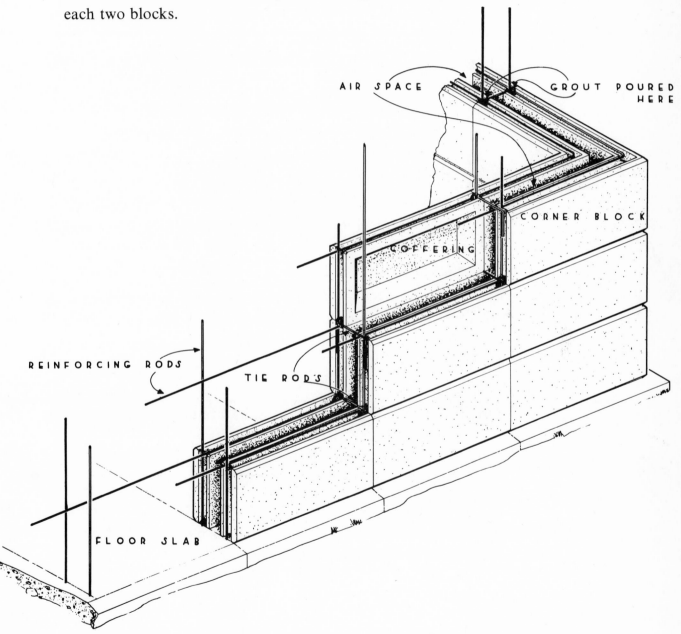

c) Grout, formed of one part cement and two parts sand, is then poured into the vertical groove at joints, running into the horizontal groove at joints locking all into a solid mass.

d) Horizontal rods are laid in horizontal grooves as the courses are laid up.

e) If double walls are planned, galvanized U-shaped wall tie-rods are set at each joint to anchor outer and inner block-walls to each other.

f) Another course of blocks is set upon the one now already poured.

g) As each course is added, grout is again poured into vertical joints, automatically filling the previous horizontal joint at the same time. Etc. Etc.

The pattern, design and size of the blocks may vary greatly. In some cases blocks have been made with patterned holes into which glass (sometimes colored) is set. When these glazed perforated units are assembled they form a translucent grille or screen of concrete, glass and steel.

At corners special monolithic corner blocks are used; in the case of double walls inside and outside corner blocks are required. About nine various types of block are needed to complete the house, most of them made from the same mold. For ceilings the same block units have been employed to cast horizontal ceiling and roof slabs, the same reinforcing rods forming a reinforced slab on which to put built up roofing above.

In this "Usonian Automatic" we have eliminated the need for skilled labor by prefabricating all plumbing, heating and wiring, so each appurtenance system may come into the building in a factory-made package, easily installed by making several simple connections provided during block-construction.

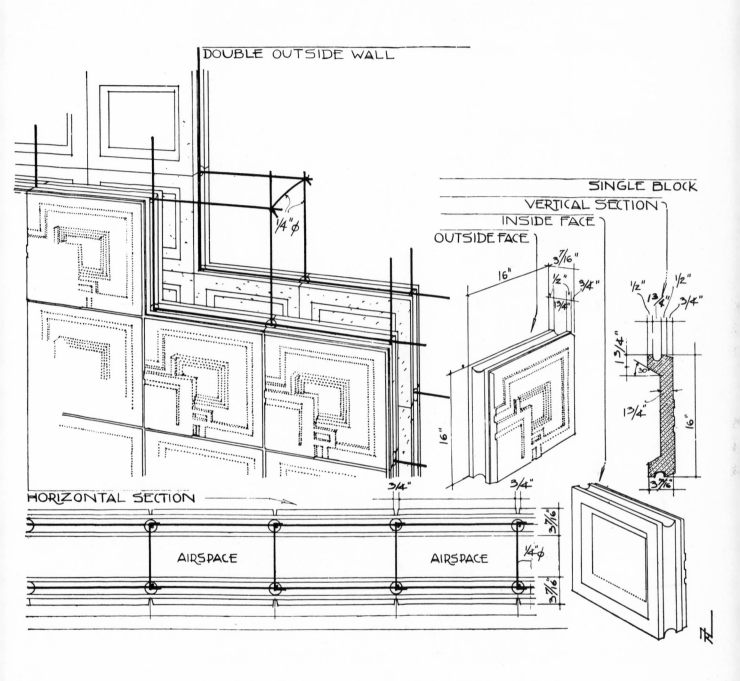

DOUBLE OUTSIDE WALL

¼"∅

SINGLE BLOCK
VERTICAL SECTION
INSIDE FACE
OUTSIDE FACE

16"

3⁷⁄₁₆"
½"
¾"
1¾"

½"
1¾"
¾"

½"
1¾"

16"

1¾"

30°

13¾"

16"

3⁷⁄₁₆"

HORIZONTAL SECTION

AIRSPACE

AIRSPACE

3/4"

3/4"

3⁷⁄₁₆"

¼"∅

3⁷⁄₁₆"

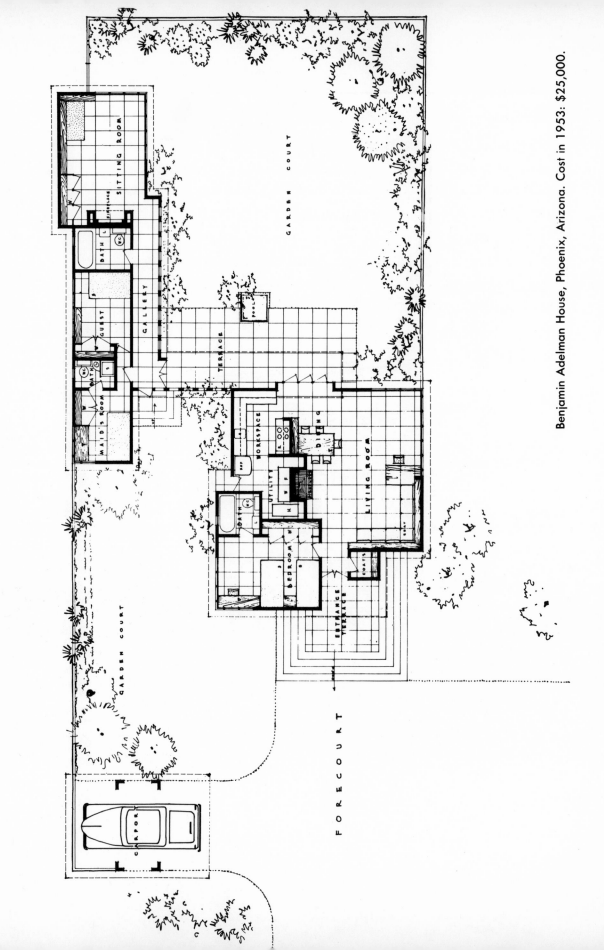

Benjamin Adelman House, Phoenix, Arizona. Cost in 1953: $25,000.

Here then, within moderate means for the free man of our democracy, with some intelligence and by his own energy, comes a natural house designed in accordance with the principles of organic architecture. A house that may be put to work in our society and give us an architecture for "housing" which is becoming to a free society because, though standardized fully, it yet establishes the democratic ideal of variety—the sovereignty of the individual. A true architecture may evolve. As a consequence conformation does not mean stultification but with it imagination may devise and build freely for residential purposes an immensely flexible varied building in groups never lacking in grace or desirable distinction.

USONIAN AUTOMATIC—ADELMAN HOUSE, PHOENIX, ARIZONA.

Dining area and workspace beyond, seen from living room. Glazed doors to garden on right.

(below) View toward south from garden court of Adelman House. Glazed doors to living room at left, glazed concrete screen along gallery to guest wing at right.

Detail. Gallery in guest wing. Entry to guest sitting room at far end.

(below) View toward south over garden wall, living room at left, guest sitting room at right.

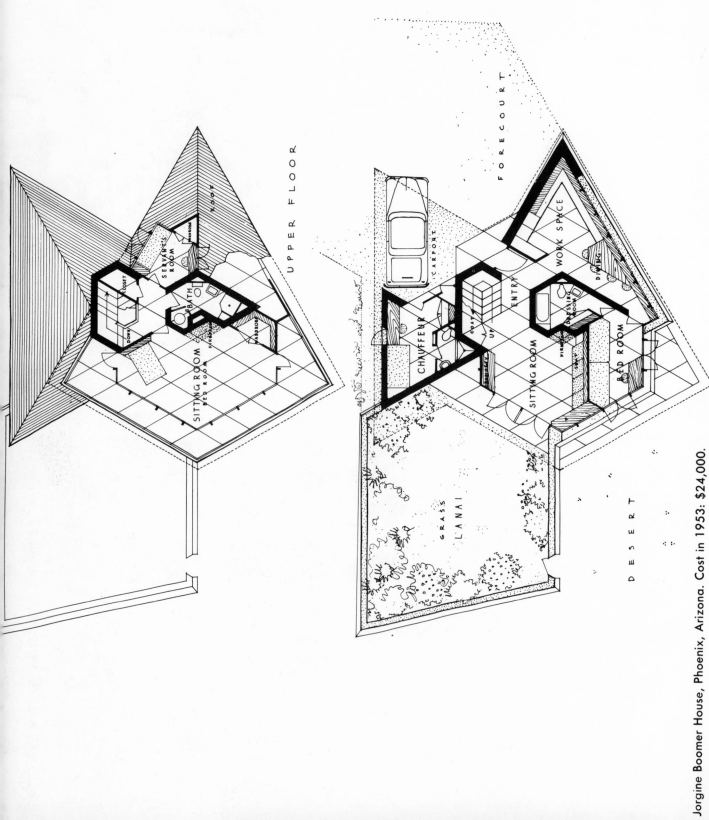

UPPER FLOOR

FORECOURT

CARPORT

CHAUFFEUR

ENTRY

WORK SPACE

SITTING ROOM

BED ROOM

GRASS LANAI

DESERT

SERVANT'S ROOM

BATH

SITTING ROOM
BED ROOM

Jorgine Boomer House, Phoenix, Arizona. Cost in 1953: $24,000.

BOOMER HOUSE, PHOENIX, ARIZONA. VIEW TOWARD WEST.

View from northeast. Walls are of rough blocks of red desert stone set in concrete.

(below) View toward south, glazed walls of sitting room reflecting mountain view.

(above) View from southwest, showing patterned
windows of dining area and workspace.

Carport, seen from west. Entrance to chauffeur's
quarters below wide overhanging eaves.

BOOMER HOUSE, PHOENIX, ARIZONA. VIEW FROM SOUTHEAST.

ORGANIC ARCHITECTURE

AND THE ORIENT

When I built the Imperial Hotel in Tokyo, Japan, I tried to make a coherent link between what the Japanese then were on their knees and what they now wanted to be on their feet. Every civilization that had gone to Japan had looted their culture. Because it was the only such genuine culture, coming from their own ground as it did, I was determined as an American to take off my hat to that extraordinary culture. At the same time I was now faced with the problem of how to build a modern building earthquake-proof.

This was mainly the Mikado's building. So I had also to consider the Mikado's needs for a social clearing house for the official life that would inevitably now come to Japan. So the Impeho would have to be comfortable enough for foreigners, although primarily it would need to serve the needs of the Japanese.

That became quite a problem—in addition to the earthquake which we never lost sight of day or night. The seismograph in Japan is never still. At night you have the feeling that the bed is going down under you and you are lost. You never get rid of that nice feeling.

But across the moat just beyond, there was the Emperor's

Palace, and since I was the Emperor's "Kenchikaho" (High Builder) and he was really my client, I felt impelled to devise ways and means not too far removed from what would be becoming to that palace of his across the moat. I think I succeeded. It is all there so far as it could be done at the time.

Of course, when I wanted to use native materials for the building—the common stone that was underfoot in Tokyo, called *oya*, which is something like travertine with big, burned, brown spots in it— there was a terrific objection by the building committee. Too common. But I liked the material and finally won. We built with "oya." We could use it by the acre—which we proceeded to do. We bought whole quarries far up at Nikko, so we quarried it there and floated it down to the site—in great barges.

The problem was how to help the Japanese people up from their knees and onto their feet. That problem still remained. When the Japanese had selected foreign things to live with, they had taken our most obvious forms which are our worst. They were uncomfortable at awkward high tables, and when sitting on the high chairs suitable to us their short legs would dangle. The first thing to do then was to get everything down to their own human-scale so that they could sit on a chair with their feet on the floor, eat at tables that did not require them to sit with food just under their chins. Sleep in beds up off the floor. Thus, to start with, the whole scale of the building became Japanese.

The next problem was how to devise things that were in reasonable accord with their high state of civilization. Instead of making so many things that would simply stand around, the way we have them, everything began to have its own place in its own way—to be put away out of sight when not wanted—the living areas kept clear. For example, the dressing table became just a mirror against the wall with a little movable cabinet against the wall beside it. It could be moved around and a chair belonging to the room could be brought up to sit there beside it. All such things I simplified in accordance with Japanese culture so far as possible, making them easy and natural for Japanese use. At the same time, everything must have true esthetic effect and be not too impractical for the foreigner.

The Japanese had never had interior bathrooms or toilets. They had what they called the "benjo," and the benjo had to be kept out of the "devil's corner." What was the devil's corner? It was only that corner from which the prevailing winds blew, bringing the scent from the benjo. But now in the Imperial Hotel these little detached toilet rooms became organic features of the building. And in these little bathrooms, floor heat was born. The tub was of tiles and sunk in the floor; the tile was a small vitreous mosaic and you would come out of the tub with a print of the mosaic designs on your backside. But that didn't matter.

Anyhow, it was all becoming one thing—the things within it in relation to each other—organic. The heating pipes ran across the wall above the tubs and so became a gleaming hot towel rack on which the towel would naturally dry very quickly. It was a very pretty thing to look at too, one of those bathrooms, modern but also quite in the Japanese way of doing things.

Their way of doing things was always more or less organic. The Japanese house is the closest thing to our organic house of anything ever built. They already had the instinct of adapting and *incorporating* everything, so that is one reason why I brought into the Imperial Hotel this incorporation of everything in it. The heating was in the center of the room in a little hand-wrought filigree copper tower, on top of which was a light fixture that spread light over the ceiling—indirect lighting. The beds were one this way and one that way, at right angles, and to one side in their center was a nest of small tables that could be decentralized and spread around the room—all more or less organic in itself, again like their own arrangements at home.

Finally we used to go around to determine the impact of the building on "the foreign guest." We would see these fellows come in with their trunks and bags—accompanied by the timid little Japanese house-boy—the boy apologetic and bowing them in, trying to show them everything (how this should be, how they should do that). The "guest" would come up and perhaps kick the table nest in the center and say, "What the hell do you call this?" and "Where is the telephone?" and "Where do these things go?"

Well, the utility all went into appropriate closets provided for them. Everything was there but everything was absorbed, and so puzzled them. The little Japanese boy would be very kindly and apologetic for everything that existed. But the whole attitude of the American tourist was: "Well, what do you know? Now, what the hell do you call this?" Etc., etc., etc.

THE PHILOSOPHY AND THE DEED

Many people have wondered about an Oriental quality they see in my work. I suppose it is true that when we speak of organic architecture, we are speaking of something that is more Oriental than Western. The answer is: my work *is,* in that deeper philosophic sense, Oriental. These ideals have not been common to the whole people of the Orient; but there was Laotse, for instance. Our society has never known the deeper Taoist mind. The Orientals must have had the sense of it, whatever may have been their consideration for it, and they instinctively built that way. Their instinct was right. So this gospel of organic architecture still has more in sympathy and in common with Oriental thought than it has with any other thing the West has ever confessed.

The West as "the West" had never known or cared to know much about it. Ancient Greece came nearest—perhaps—but not very close, and since the later Western civilizations in Italy, France, England and the United States went heavily—stupidly—Greek in their architecture, the West could not easily have seen an indigenous organic architecture. The civilizations of India, Persia, China and Japan are all based on the same central source of cultural inspiration, chiefly Buddhist, stemming from the original inspiration of his faith. But it is not so much the principles of this faith which underlie organic architecture, as the faith of Laotse—the Chinese philosopher—his annals preserved in Tibet. But I became conscious of these only after I had found and built it for myself.

And yet the West cannot hope to have anything original unless by individual inspiration. Our culture is so far junior and so far outclassed in time by all that we call Oriental. You will surely find that nearly everything we stand for today, everything we think of as originated by us, is thus old. To make matters in our new nation worse, America has always assumed that culture, to be culture, had to come from European sources—be imported. The idea of an organic architecture, therefore, coming from the tall grass of the Midwestern American prairie, was regarded at home as unacceptable. So it went around the world to find recognition and then to be "imported" to its own home as a thing to be imitated everywhere, though the understanding of its principles has never yet really caught up with the penetration of the original deed at home.

It cannot truthfully be said, however, that organic architecture was derived from the Orient. We have our own way of putting these elemental (so ancient) ideals into practical effect. Although

Laotse, as far as we know, first enunciated the philosophy, it probably preceded him but was never built by him or any Oriental. The idea of organic architecture that the reality of the building lies in the space within to be lived in, the feeling that we must not enclose ourselves in an envelope which is the building, is not alone Oriental. Democracy, proclaiming the integrity of the individual *per se,* had the feeling if not the words. Nothing else Western except the act of an organic architecture had ever happened to declare that Laotsian philosophic principle which was declared by him 500 years before our Jesus. It is true that the wiser, older civilizations of the world had a quiescent sense of this long before we of the West came to it.

For a long time, I thought I had "discovered" it, only to find after all that this idea of the interior space being the reality of the building was ancient and Oriental. It came to me quite naturally from my Unitarian ancestry and the Froebelian kindergarten training in the deeper primal sense of the form of the interior or heart of the appearance of "things." I was entitled to it by the way I happened to come up along the line—perhaps. I don't really know. Chesty with all this, I was in danger of thinking of myself as, more or less, a prophet. When building Unity Temple at Oak Park and the Larkin Building in Buffalo, I was making the first great protest I knew anything about against the building coming up on you from the outside as enclosure. I reversed that old idiom in idea and in fact.

When pretty well puffed up by this I received a little book by Okakura Kakuzo, entitled *The Book of Tea,* sent to me by the ambassador from Japan to the United States. Reading it, I came across this sentence: "The reality of a room was to be found in the space enclosed by the roof and walls, not in the roof and walls themselves."

Well, there was I. Instead of being the cake I was not even dough. Closing the little book I went out to break stone on the road, trying to get my interior self together. I was like a sail coming down; I had thought of myself as an original, but was not. It took me days to swell up again. But I began to swell up again when I thought, "After all, who built it? Who put that thought into buildings? Laotse nor anyone had consciously *built* it." When I thought of that, naturally enough I thought, "Well then, everything is all right, we can still go along with head up." I have been going along—head up—ever since.

ACKNOWLEDGMENTS

SOURCES

The first chapter, on Organic Architecture, appeared originally in The Architect's Journal of London, 1936. The chapters, Building the New House, In the Nature of Materials: A Philosophy, The Usonian House I and II, are quoted from "An Autobiography," published by Duell, Sloan and Pearce, copyright 1943 by Frank Lloyd Wright. Concerning the Usonian House was written in 1953; all other chapters written for this book by Mr. Wright in 1954.

PHOTOGRAPHERS' CREDITS

L. J. CUNEO: 85, 87
DAVID DAVISON: 153, 171 (top), 173, 174
DAVID DODGE: 163, 201, 205
P. E. GUERRERO: 88, 90, 117, 118, 124, 134, 176
HEDRICH-BLESSING: 71, 72, 73, 74, 75, 76, 103, 145, 146
JACK HOWE: 157, 185
ROBERT IMANDT: 93, 94, 95
G. E. KIDDER-SMITH: 111, 112, 113
HERMAN KROLL: 171 (bottom), 172
LEAVENWORTH'S: 105
HELEN LEVITT: Portrait of Frank Lloyd Wright, 199, 200
JOE MUNROE: 104
MARC NEUHOF: 189, 190, 191, 192, 193, 194
EZRA STOLLER: 120, 122, 123, 125, 132, 133, 135, 137
EDMUND TESKE: 136
L. S. WILLIS: 107

Taliesin team of apprentices on construction of Usonian Exhibition House: John de Koven Hill, Curtis Besinger, Kenn Lockhart, John Geiger, Robin Molny, Kelly Oliver, Edmund Thomas Casey, Morton Delson, John Rattenbury, Edward Thurman, James Pfefferkorn, George Thompson, Herbert De Levie, David Wheatley.